MW01608170

PRELUDE TO DISASTER

Deconstruction of Our Educational System and Our Society

JOHN V. PATRICK

PublishAmerica
Baltimore

Hardcover 978-1-4560-4111-3
Softcover 978-1-4560-4112-0
PUBLISHED BY PUBLISHAMERICA, LLLP
www.publishamerica.com
Baltimore

Printed in the United States of America

CONTENTS

INTRODUCTION *and* FOREWORD

Civilization is a descriptive term for a relatively complex agricultural and urban culture and can be distinguished from other cultures by its high level of social complexity and organization, and by their diverse economic and cultural activities.

I am not sure how this concept of civilization began but it definitely connotes that comparisons must be made and progress within the culture is measured relative to our interpretations of these comparisons. Unfortunately, we have developed beliefs where comparisons based on the demise and demonization of others is the norm and most promising road to cultural success. Those who have benefited the most from practices driven by these beliefs are beginning to accelerate our culture towards a un-sustainable and dogmatic way of life. We must reverse this trend. We must un-learn the belief that we are better because we have made others weaker and learn to grow from within ourselves. We, as a people, must rid ourselves of these neurotic obsessions derived from the other people effect.

Thru education, we must teach ourselves that we can only be better when we gain the love and respect of others. And, we must teach ourselves how to love and respect each other for in the competitive games of winning and losing, half will lose half the games. And, when the losers become ineffective, our society will eventually regress to zero.

Education, in the largest sense, is any act or experience that has a formative effect on the mind character or physical ability of an individual. In its technical sense, education is the process by which society deliberately transmits its accumulated knowledge, skills and values from one generation to another (Wikipedia). By any reasonable evaluation our system of education has moved backwards. Our position as a leader in the industrial world is in serious jeopardy and the character and sustainability of our democracy has been reduced to the questionable category.

Puzzled by experiences as a high school chemistry teacher, research chemist turned teacher, John V. Patrick set out to develop and rationalize of his experiences as a teacher. In his first book "Prelude to Chaos" author John V. Patrick suggested that students bred by our society are a bunch of defiant, anti-establishment neurotics who are so disruptive that our teachers cannot teach them and were driving our society to chaos.

In this, his second book, "A Prelude to Disaster, the deconstructing our schools and society", his classroom experiences are more explicit and so is his rational of factors leading to the demise of our education system, and to societal drift towards a more dogmatic mentality. Although his description of classroom experiences yields compassion for teachers, he points more directly at the failure of teachers for not exerting a greater influence, on our school system and on our societal drift towards dogmatic endeavors.

More dramatic are his thoughts on how society with its inner regulating mentality has augmented drift towards a more dogmatic society and the affect it has had on our education system and the authorities that regulate it. His proposed solutions thru the teaching of self-actualization are more logically detailed and convincingly practical. Especially convincing is his fresh look at the inner-self as a taming mechanism for our dogmatic drift.

His approach to traits such as, aggressiveness verses competitive dogma, failure verses strategic complacency, advancement verses stagnation; all related to his description of self-actualization of the inner self, are thought provoking. Although counterintuitive, his approach is convincingly realistic.

Patrick draws heavily from diverse life experiences as a learned citizen, research chemist, teacher and educational researcher, all shrouded in descriptive lessons from the school of hard knocks, to present a logical and convincing scenario of a prelude to disaster and its possible remedies.

CHAPTER I

The New Teacher

As an over the hill chemist entering a new profession in which I had been warned would be challenging, I did not know what to expect. I had taught youngsters at a junior-senior high school for one year, about 30 years ago before entering the industrial world in search of fame and fortune. After a suggestion from a friend, I applied for this job about a week ago and since there was such a shortage of chemistry teachers, I was hired on the spot with hardly any additional teacher training or time to really consider this job or continue looking for something different. My one year of teaching experience seemed like a hundred years ago. On my application, I noted that I had completed a course titled "Techniques in Military Instruction". Now, here I am standing in front of a high school chemistry class waiting for the first class of the year and of my new career to begin.

As my first student entered, my mind could not help but flash back to my first teaching job—30 some years ago. She was a fairly attractive girl, a little on the heavy side but tall with light tan skin, and obvious African American features. What caused the flash back was her amazing remembrance of a student from my previous teaching job. This time she was wearing a modest outfit with a skirt about 12 inches shorter than I felt it should have been. I greeted her with a "Welcome to Chemistry" and she returned my greeting but with a smile that could melt Mount Rushmore. She did not immediately take a seat but appeared to wander about the class as if to be extremely selective of her seat. I later found that she was indeed the daughter of a student from my previous stint at teaching.

The second student to enter was also African American. A tall clean cut young man wearing what appeared to be a military uniform without any insignia. It was clean and fresh. It was obvious that he had taken great effort to fit and groom his appearance. I could not help but notice that his attire was frayed around the edges of his collar and sleeve as if it was well worn. His greeting was first and courteous but exhibited an air of unexplainable uncertainty—"Good morning sir, I am William Jones, III but everyone calls me Tray. My grand paw was William Jones I, my dad was number II, and I am number III. He was the type I welcomed into the class as he reminded me of my self, once upon a time—proud, slightly arrogant, alert, and more eager to teach rather than learn. I thought he would be challenging but fun to teach.

I particularly noticed several other students as they entered the class. A five foot two—250 pounder moon walked into the class with a grace that would have made Michael Jackson envious of him. He was known as "Woody". Then there was the shy white girl with the whitest skin I had ever seen. She took a seat in the rear of the class. She was known as Snow Flake. I was almost blown away when a skinny—six foot five with arms almost down to his knees, dribbled a basketball into class and took a seat next to Snow Flake. He was known as "Slinky". It was a rather cool morning and I particularly noticed that the next student entered wearing an overcoat. He removed it to reveal a muscle shirt and biceps that would make Mike Tyson look normal. He also was about six-five except about two thirds of his body was legs. I learned shortly that he held the state record in the 200 and 400 meter runs and was known as "High Pockets". I had to smile to myself thinking that his ass was climbing to his shoulders. For sure his good qualities were stamina and determination. My past experience told me that when you ran the 400, you blew all you had in the first 150 yards. The rest was sheer determination and mind over substance. He took a seat on the other side of Snowflake. As other student entered the class I was struck by how animated they were with each other; exhibiting theatrics somewhere between what I considered normal playful kids and the famous comic "Chris Rock. They were more racially diverse than expected. The Spanish males appeared to be somewhat more clannish, even separating themselves by skin color. Yet they did not appear to be overly obsessed with racial tensions. The females were less selective. This I could not quite understand either.

I did notice another short skirt. This one was unevenly hemmed with tape and the hem was not pressed. It appeared as if it was shortened on the way to school. Somehow I felt that her parents would not approve of her new skirt length.

I was pleased that my former student's daughter had taken a seat on the front row, but did not know what to do when she uncrossed her legs. Sitting sort of wide legged, she revealed 100 percent beaver. With a smirk she look me dead in the eyes and said "What are you looking at old man", then let loose with that smile again. I had been advised by an assigned mentor not be surprised at anything and not to appear startled or hurt by anything I saw. He did not come close to preparing me for what I had just seen. One thing I concluded was that her actions were contrived—a bit playful but not meant to hurt. Somehow I was more hurt that she referred to me as old than the other part of her theatrics. Her motives were not clear to me but, after pushing pornographic thoughts from my mind, I felt that I should try to help and understand her. Her name was Kooky.

I found later that the antics were somewhat common with her. I finally arrived home to a big plate of spicy chicken cooked in mushroom sauce over noodles. It smoothed my sole. I will never adequately explain the emotions I experienced my first day of high school teaching after 30 years as a research chemist.

I decided to not take any direct action on the Kooky incident but later did talk to an administrator about it. He was more amused than concerned by the incident and advised me to not get him involved. The school did have a dress code in place that regulated dress length and outlawed muscle shirts. I was a bit taken back because the administrator had opted to not get involved with the Kooky no panties incident. However, I found later that most administrators were passive on problems, especially problems that reeked of controversy. They ran from most problems that they were not forced to get involved with.

Several days later, an uneasy feeling set in the pit of my stomach. As the bell rung for the start of the class, Snow Flake had changed her seat from between the two Jocks and several students wondered in as much as 15 minutes late with bags of McDonald's breakfast which they spread on their desk as if they were at home and preparing to enjoy a leisurely meal. Several other students began begging to share their food as if they were starving. They appeared angry when the students did not shear with them. I had prepared a set of class rules consisting mostly of lab policies and safety concerns which I had planned to hand out but decided to wait and modify them to include the many other issues that needed addressing. One of my most urgent tasks was to attempt to arrange the student seating in alphabetical order because it was obvious that they had seated themselves in groups of playful clans. While attempting to reseat the students, I found out quickly that they would only identify themselves with their nick names rather than their sir names. Re-seating was a playful game for them resulting in only a slight modification of the original fun orientated groups. I noticed that that they often mocked each other, sometimes with what appeared to me as blatant cruelty. For example one might blurt out, "I am not sitting by him. He stinks, or has bad breath. Sometimes the excuses were toned down. Such as, "she needs a mouth wash, or somebody has to give this fool give a mint before I set by him. Woody has to take his hands out of his pocket and go wash his hands. I bet he does not have real pockets in those paints—that is why they call him Woody.

A habit and hobby of mine was to always attempt to analyze everything, but mostly physical things, especially when they were considered unusual. It wasn't long before I realized that my habit was extended to people, mostly students. This was my internal attempt at developing tolerance. Plus, I have a basic fear of people I felt were abnormal or crazy. My first thought was that their actions were an attempt to test me as a new teacher. But somehow, this did not correlate. Their actions appeared more deep seated and more individually personal. Sometimes, the student on the blunt end of their putdowns seemed to enjoy the putdown and would even retaliate with a counter putdown, provoking more disruption and laughter from other students. Examples of retaliation might be "Your mama has bad breath" or even worst "I gave your mama her bad breath". I was practically amazed at so much emphasis and references to sex—their dress, the sexual innuendos and conversations.

Dumfounded, I let this sort of thing continue for a while as I stalled more and more for the bell to ring. I tried to be indifferent to what was going on and thought to myself, what a wasted day. My first lesson at acquiescing to student's desires had been realized. They were winning the first battles and I felt it was going to be a long war, yet an interesting year for me.

On my way home, I was in a daze and ended up about two exits past my turn off as my thoughts flashed back to my high school days when games called "Playing the dozens" was common. The idea was to put someone down with words. I cannot tell when or how these games originated. There were groups of students that loved playing these type games and there were those that did not. Some loved to just listen and laugh while some feared them. About a year ago there was a reasonably popular TV show called "Your Mama" where contestants would crack jokes about their opponents' mama and a panel of judges would determine the winner by whose jokes were the funniest. The TV show was amazingly similar to what happened in my class, even though the show was produced many years afterwards.

As I tried to rationalize the day's events, especially the seating and silly putdown game episodes, my thoughts turned to egos and what I remembered from my psychology class as super egos. As a kid, we had lots of fun with what we called "Playing the Dozens"—a game where we deliberately put each other down with words. In all episodes of these games the object was to degrade, sometimes using jokes that were brutally spiteful. The jokes were penetrating, personal and, more than a few times, resulted in fights. The classroom episodes were extreme puzzling to me because I did not feel the spitefulness and rudeness was deliberately directed towards me neither as a teacher nor to their fellow student on the receiving end of the joke. The targeted students appeared to be randomly selected even though one would often wonder if they had any bases of fact. Unscientifically, I concluded that the game was instigated to booster the super ego of the instigator. I thought puzzlingly, why anyone would go to so much trouble, risk starting a fight or risk losing a friend or inciting the wrath of their teacher, only for a few minutes of boosted ego. I figured something had to be missing from their lives—something big and important. I thought that ego bolstering activities were fairly common, took various forms and intensities, and were amazing clever- and exhibited a certain amount of creativity. They were mostly funny but ate at my inner sense of responsibility as a teacher.

While continuing to ponder the puzzling events, my thoughts turned to religion and the events at last Sunday's church service, more so to my memory of the musical lyrics which had resonated with me. I had remembered how intense and emotional the congregation became as they uttered the words of the songs—"He walks with me and he talks with me and he tells me I am his own", "Crown thy good with brotherhood", and "Bless be the tide that binds". What I thought with my scientific mind suggested a common theme of comradery—the desire to belong. And the strength associated with belonging was a source of salvation and strength. The desire to belong was a strong factor creating the emotions, I thought. This type of thinking reinforced my belief that ego was a strong driving force creating a strong inner sanctuary for my students, causing them to attack each other with a spiteful revenge, especially if the desire to belong was not being fulfilled and was a perceived deficiency which needed correcting. Their objective was not to hurt but to create laughter and a feeling of being accepted, somewhat like a comedian on a stage seeking laughter—the more laughter, the greater the acceptance. In my search for answers, I came across a passage I liked. It is related to ego but called "Neurotic Pride", in Karen Horney's "Neurosis and Human Growth":

Following is the quote I liked.

"The pernicious character of neurotic pride lies in the combination of it being vitally important to the individual and at the same time rendering him extremely vulnerable. This situation (egocentric deficiencies) creates tensions, which because of their frequency and intensity are so unbearable that they call for remedies: automatic endives to restore pride when it is hurt and to avoid injuries when it is endangered.

The need to save face is urgent, and there is more than one way of affecting it, gross and subtle. The most effective and it seems, almost ubiquitous one is interlocked with the impulse to take revenge for what is felt as humiliation. It is a reaction of hostility to the pain and the danger involved in a hurt pride. Vindictiveness may be, in addition, a means towards self-vindication. It involves the belief that by getting back at the offender one's own pride may be restored. This belief is based on the feeling that the offender, by his very power to hurt another's pride, has put himself above his victim and has defeated him. By taking revenge and hurting him more, the situation will be reversed. The aim of the vindictive revenge is not getting even, but to triumph by hitting back harder. Nothing short of triumph can restore the imaginary grandeur in which pride is invested. It is this very capacity to restore pride that gives vindictiveness its incredible tenacity and accounts for its compulsive character".

This passage fit my developing theory very well but I questioned how could so many kids be suffering from the same malady? To be pried driven is good. Why was I considering it a malady? What the hell I thought— ego, neurotic pride, and belonging—they all fit well into

17

Horney's theory. These kids are not learning and I and apparently no one else, really knows why. And, far too many do not care.

My department chair had presented me with a course of study which consisted essentially of the table of contents from a ten year old chemistry text book and advised me that two days per week was lab days and students were expected to perform hands on lab experiments—a directive from downtown because students needed more hands on work rather than what was commonly known as "Chalk and Talk", where the teacher lectured and wrote stuff on the chalkboard. For a chemistry class, the students interpreted this as, and coined the phrase, "Burn and learn".

Another big surprise was that my laboratory classroom had no working water, electricity or gas. The first unit I was to teach was titled "The Scientific Method". Realizing that this was the same title of units taught in some form in every science class since first grade, I opted for something I felt was a little more creative, hopefully more challenging, but still exhibiting the scientific method. I developed a unit demonstrating how the individual variables in a multi variable experiment could be separated based on their individual observable contributions to an effect within the experiment. I thought this experiment would teach other important attributes of a chemist such as patience, a sense of observation, scientific intuition and a few others lessons that needed teaching. It did not take long for me to realize that this was a violation of the "Burn and learn" idea of what chemistry was all about. Additionally, based on what I had observed about my students, I was not yet ready to purchase gas canisters with my own money, turn them loose with matches, gas and no water in the same class room.

The experiment asked "How many drops of water could be placed on a penny before the water would run off, and what were the identity and relative contribution of variables that would contribute to the maximum number of drops being placed on the penny. A two level—four variable experiment was outlined for them. The variables were (A) height of the drop, (B) location of the drop (middle or edge of the penny); (C) weather the drops were placed on the heads or tails side of the penny, and (D) weather the penny was natural or polished by sanding. The following outline of the experiment was passed out to the students and I explained to them how it should work.

Experimental Outline (Two Level Factorial Experiment)

Variable Chart

Exp number	A	B	C	D
1.	-	-	-	-
2.	+	-	-	-
3.	-	+	-	-
4.	+	-	-	-
5.	-	+	-	-
6.	+	-	+	-
7.	-	+	+	-
8.	+	+	+	+
9.	-	-	-	+
10.	+	-	-	+
11.	-	+	-	+
12.	+	+	-	+
13.	-	-	+	+

14.	+	-	+	+
15.	-	+	+	+
16	+	+	+	+

Note: Plus indicates the high (+) level and negative (-) indicated the low level of the variable.

Before I explain what happened with the experiment, let me regress to what was happening with Kooky and Snowflake.

Kooky started wearing panties. They changed from red to black, red, and pink, yellow and sometimes white. I did smile when I realized there were five colors and five school days per week. My perverted mind caused me to wonder to myself, what she wore on weekends. As I was beginning to adjust to this anomaly, one day after standing in the hall chasing students who tended to linger in the hallway into the class after the bell had wrong, I entered the classroom to find Snowflake sitting on Kooky's lap with what appeared as her tong halfway down her throat.

I was shocked out of my mind but tried to not show it. I am not sure where it came from but all I could get out was "One student to a seat please" Another student chuckled. The remainder of the class was amazingly indifferent. Snowflake rose, adjusted her skirt, let out a smile as if she was mimicking that great smile of Kooky. Snowflake's smile was so similar to Kooky's that I thought of peer pressure and how student behavior was often related to students desire to be one of the groups. Her smile was a mimic, I thought. Whenever one student did something, others would almost always follow, especially the bad actions.

What was a teacher to do with this incident? I thought about everything, all things, but deep down inside I was frightened, mostly about doing nothing. After several days I did mention this incident to my favorite do not get me involved administrator. He inform me that Snowflake's family owned several blocks of houses in the hood and probably owned the house that Kooky's family lived in. Caution was advised but no recommendation on how to handle the situation, and no recommended action I might take or should have taken came fourth. After about a week, I noticed that Kooky begin to distant herself from Snowflake and in a moment of weakness (or strength) I got up enough nerve to ask Kooky about the kissing incident. She replied, "Old man"—and this really hurt again—"You don't know anything. What was I supposed to do—throw the skinny bitch across the room"? She came onto me." I did not completely understand the rationality of what she said verses what I saw or thought I saw, but deep down inside I was relieved. I guess I wanted to believe that Kooky was really not like that. Coupled with what the administrator had told me about the housing situation, I thought their relationship might be one born out of necessity or was some sort of payoff. I walked away and wanted to kick my own ass: questioning why I was thinking about any type justification for what I had seen. Were my thoughts another case of teacher acquiescing to students—one that could not or should not be blamed on a do nothing administrator or one that I could blame someone for? I did admit to myself that I was thinking about sex a little bit more than I wanted to or should have.

I was reminded that at a school dance, 20 some years ago, Kooky's mother, then a student of mine had asked me to dance. I was a young teacher and got excited. I was sure that she did not notice it, but I did feel awkward when several other students also asked me to dance. Had she noticed and told other students? Some relief came when another teacher asked me to dance. It had to be my good looks, I thought. The dance let out early because a fight broke out in the corner of the dance hall—two girls were vacuously at each other.

My classes were not going so well. The students were complaining about the big water drop experiment which I admit was taking too long but felt it was not really my fault. They complained that it was not really chemistry and asked why they had to drop water on a penny. In spite of detailed explanations and descriptions of the experiment I felt violated.

They asked "What are we learning" I went ballistic before I explained to them for about the fifth time that the experiment teaches how to determine the relative significance of the variables being studied and what they were learning had other applications. For example if you wanted to predict the grade a student would make on a given test they could study various criteria related to the test and learning. I explained that the same technique could be used to increase the overall score of the class. But they would first have to collect data. The data, especially scientific data, could sometimes appear random and could require special analysis and techniques to unravel the apparent agglomeration of random data. I wondered if a better teacher could have explained the experiment differently or would have selected a better experiment.

I gave them the following example of three factor experiment where the (A) age of the student and (B) hours of preparation for the test, and (C) sex of the student, could be used as a two level—three variable experiment. Would you believe that Snowflake wanted to know how we would handle any third sex situations if there were any around? Her question, I thought, especially her the comment about "If there were any third sex students around" was a message to me that she was not really gay, and was only pondering with the idea. I also felt that Kooky had shared with her, the conversation we had about their kissing incident. Isn't it difficult for teachers to be objective about students? Maybe teachers should forget about this type stuff and just stick to teaching. I also thought that this type crap was clouding my mind and detracting me from teaching.

I took the time to prepare the following fake example of how the experiment was supposed to work, hoping to use the opportunity to explain a slightly different experimental version. I passed out the following set of data, results and explanation.

DATA, ANALYSIS AND RESULTS OF THE SAMPLE DATA

Experimental Design (the high and lows by variable chart) Use the variable chart to organize the data and results of the experiment.

Variables

EXP #	A	B	C	Test Score
1	13	20	Male	90
2	15	25	M	80
3	13	11	M	95
4	16	16	M	85
5	14	14	Female	60
6	17	18	F	75
7	15	20	F	95
8	16	10	F	85
Av	15	15	—	83

ANALYSIS OF DATA

Group Data Results
Group data according to variables, and average the results by variables

Exp# A-		Exp# A+		Exp# B-		Exp# B+	
1	90	2	80	1	90	3	95
3	95	4	85	2	80	2	80
5	60	6	75	5	60	7	95
7	95	8	85	6	75	8	85
Ave	85		81		76		90

Exp # CM		Exp# CF	
1	90	5	60
2	80	6	95
3	95	7	95
4	85	8	85
Ave	88		79 (Overall average is 83)

The projected highest test score would be those who studied the longest (B+) with an average score of 90, followed by the males(CM)with an average score of 88, then(A-) whose average score was 85)the younger students. All other variables' were negative scoring less than the overall average.

With this explanation, especially the explanation of how to analyze the individual variables, most students appeared to understand the experiment better. Kooky said, "I like this shit". I could figure out lots of stuff with this. In spite of understanding the concepts most of the students still had trouble completing the project which included completing the water drop experiment and writing a report. The report was to consist of an introduction telling what was done and why, a detailed description of how it was done, results and data to substantiate the results. See appendix 3III Guide to technical report writing which was distributed to students

One of my most difficult tasks was grading their reports. They all read the same. It rapidly became obvious that copying was rampart. A few turned in a photo copy of someone else's report with the name whited out and their own name inserted. It was somewhat encouraging that there were a few well written and documented reports—but so few that I began to give A's to half ass reports. This must have been some sort of irrational searching for good students. Most of my students voiced a strong opinion that they would rather be taught things rather than having to actually do them or actually learn things themselves. "Just teach us", was their favorite suggestion, presented in a complaining manor.

CHAPTER II

The Students

Their objections, about almost everything, kicked into high gear and my mind kicked into the research mode, trying to figure out what all this meant. I felt a bit depressed because only a few students would qualify, even potentially, as good chemistry students. I concluded that the students were not accustomed to the discipline of chemistry or had the patients to do a meticulous detailed experiment or expend the effort to figure out and understand a complex concept. Additionally, they were not accustomed to demanding teachers, especially ones that demanded mental discipline and critical thinking. Generally, I felt the students liked to learn and wanted to learn. But, under the stress imposed by the difficulty of learning, which they were not accustomed to, they would rebel, give-up, or revert to an easier subject that would afford them greater and more rapid self-actualization or to some other remedy for their frustrations such as joking around. I did not feel they were lazy. In their quest for self-actualization or recognition, they resorted to jokes, open defiance, finagling, and lying, cheating and even bribery. My thinking suggested that ego is encapsulated in their quest for self-actualization. Their deprived self-actualizations would lead to irrational thoughts and actions. All of this was a head full, even for my own image of my analytical mind.

I came across the picture of the kitty cat looking in the mirror and saw a lion. I thought about what would happen if the image was reversed—if the lion was looking in the mirror and saw a pussy cat. Could Kooky be suffering from low self-esteem, causing her to display her wares? How could she have ever grown to accept such actions as normal and acceptable?

Woody had gained after school employment at a local meat market. One day I went in and purchased a third pound of pastrami. He served me with pride and I noticed an unusually broad smile as he handed me my pastrami with a wink. As I arrived home I noticed I had about three times the pastrami that I ordered and paid for. I thought he liked me as a teacher but was still naively puzzled until he approached me somewhat angrily after I returned his quiz paper with an F and said, "When are you going to hook me up?" Then I realized that the extra pastrami was a bribe. My naivety flashed before me and I wondered what else I had not realized was a bribe—the smiles, placates and other favors. How did all this relate to the hostility I had experienced from the students? How much had I been manipulated by students? A fellow male teacher was caught having sex with a student. I also remembered that a parent had told me that she did not like the idea of an English teacher picking up her son for tutoring in her home at night. Was I being forced to think about sex or was it me? The students appeared to be more obsessed with it, I thought.

I am not sure where or when the negative learning habits begin, but it had to be at an early age. Classical educational theory blames all sorts of things for these poor habits of learning. To name a few there are low income families, a lack of parental involvement in the child's education, ineffective and undemanding teachers, and ineffective curriculum to name a few. And, they are all definitely correct to various degrees. It is interesting to note that the list is almost void of manipulative, conniving, defiant and hostile students. High on my list of causes of poor learning, I thought, is a lack of discipline. Even though underestimated as a cause of poor learning, educational theorist blames lack of discipline on poor pedagogy and classroom management problems. It is interesting that most teachers will tell you that bad students produce classroom management problems while most administrators will say it is poor classroom management that causes discipline problems. Until now, I had not thought of poor mental discipline as a source of poor learning habits. It was obvious to me that outward discipline problems were increasing, is a major problem and like all types of poor learning habits is increasing in all schools, including suburban and private schools.

Summarizing my theories about this gigantic dilemma I came up with the following list and concluded that the factors are no doubt interactive to a large extent.

1. The basic problem of students not being driven to learn, especially difficult subject matter, is a societal phenomenon, presently concentrated in inner cities but rapidly spreading and increasing in the suburbs, including our elite private schools.

2. The rapid spread of our demising habit of poor learning is enhanced by a generational effect—a deep seeded belief that success is enhanced by manipulations, luck

and circumstances of which individuals feel they have no control over. This belief and its affect are enhanced when passed from one generation to the next **generation to the next. The context of this affect is to survive by any means possible.**

3. A deep seated fear that other people create our demise is rapidly increasing. And, it is this conjecture and its relation to our egos that is most detrimental. We all want to succeed and feel bad when we do not. A feeling that others are the cause of our problems leads to a drive towards vindictive triumph. Here, we want to defeat and humiliate others by putting them to shame through our own success (Karen Horney). It is also a strong driving force behind our competitive drive.

4. Ego, fear of failure, shame, and pride are all emotion based factors which affect the quality of our thinking and how we learn and how we relate to each other.

I am not sure why I started to read. Maybe it was my research background or just life experiences that led me to Horney. As usual, I begin to apply my own analysis and situations to what I was reading.

In her book Self-Analysis (1942), Horney outlined the 10 neurotic needs she had identified and the traits associated with the needs:

1. **The Neurotic Need for Affection and Approval**

This needs include the desires to be liked, to please other people, and meet the expectations of others. People with this type of need are extremely sensitive to rejection and criticism and fear the anger or hostility of others. This need may definitely be related to ego and can damage attitudes when denied.

2. **The Neurotic Need for a Partner Who Will Take over One's Life**

   These involve the need to be centered on a partner. People with this need suffer extreme fear of being abandoned by their partner. Oftentimes, these individuals place an exaggerated importance on love and believe that having a partner will resolve all of life's troubles. In the urban schools, especially at the middle school level, disruptions caused by friendships, jealousy or lovers quails, and immature sex problems are common phenomena.

3. **The Neurotic Need to restrict one's Life within Narrow Borders**

   Individuals with this need prefer to remain inconspicuous and unnoticed. They are undemanding and content with little. They avoid wishing for material things, often making their own needs secondary and undervaluing their own talents and abilities. Shy and apparently timid students are common to this need. This neurotic need is, although valid is no doubt more the consequence of denied self-actualization.

4. **The Neurotic Need for Power**

   Individuals with this need seek power for its own sake. They usually praise strength, despise weakness, and will exploit or dominate other people. These people fear personal limitations, helplessness, and uncontrollable situations.

5. **The Neurotic Need to Exploit Others**

   These individuals view others in terms of what can be gained through association with them. People with this need generally pride themselves in their ability to exploit other people and are often focused on manipulating others to obtain desired objectives, including such things as ideas, power, money, or sex.

6. **The Neurotic Need for Prestige**
   Individuals with a need for prestige value themselves in terms of public recognition and acclaim. Material possessions, personality characteristics professional accomplishments, and loved ones are evaluated based upon prestige value. These individuals often fear public embarrassment and loss of social status (denied self-actualization).

7. **The Neurotic Need for Personal Admiration**
   Individuals with a neurotic need for personal admiration are narcissistic and have an exaggerated self-perception. They want to be admired based on this imagined self-view, not upon how they really are.

8. **The Neurotic Need for Personal Achievement**
   According to Horney, people push themselves to achieve greater and greater things as a result of basic insecurity. These individuals fear failure and feel a constant need to accomplish more than other people and to top even their own earlier successes.

9. **The Neurotic Need for Self-Sufficiency and Independence**
   These individuals exhibit a "loner" mentality, distancing themselves from others in order to avoid being tied down or dependent upon other people.

10. **The Neurotic Need for Perfection and Unassailability**
    These individuals constantly strive for complete infallibility. A common feature of this neurotic need is searching for personal flaws in order to quickly change or cover up these perceived imperfections.

"According to Horney, basic anxiety (and therefore neurosis) could result from a variety of things including, "… direct or indirect domination, indifference, erratic behavior, lack of respect for the child's individual needs, lack of real guidance, disparaging attitudes, too much admiration or the absence of it, lack of reliable warmth, having to take sides in parental disagreements, too much or too little responsibility, over-protection, isolation from other children, injustice, discrimination, unkempt promises, hostile atmosphere, and so on and so on.

Actually, I felt that Horney's concepts were correct but a bit shallow with respect to the whole sociality picture and a little too specific for the analysis of the agglomerate of issues involved with the multitudes of factors related to school issues. But, If Horney is remotely correct I thought, one would not need to look far to find these factors, reasonably related to what I was seeing in my classrooms, throughout our schools, and rapidly increasing in all phases of our society.

Yet, my ideas began to fall into place and I could see excellent correlation of school problems within the complex matrices of personalities and their actions.

The student's complaints about my teaching begin to increase. I sensed that the complaints were beginning to increase too rapidly and appeared to be developing as a fad. The students begin to marvel and enjoy complaining about my teaching. I sometimes joked with them about their comments. I tried to add a little diversity to the experiment by introducing interfacial tension into the experiment and challenged them to develop a toy based on surface tension. It appeared as if no matter what I tried there was absolutely no real student interest in my classes. No burn and learn was interjected because such was just not practical nor available. Occasionally, I would get a glimpse of genius and creativity from a few. I thought this was derived from my hopeful attitude.

In one class I asked a student to explain a home work problem he was assigned. He proceeded to the front of the class and started to explain how he thought the problem could be worked. I could tell that this was the first time he had seen the problem and that he thought he could develop an answer by working the problem on the spot. I liked his confidence and tried to help him towards a solution. When he realized that he had no solution, his efforts turned to theatrics. I asked him if he was going to walk the walk or just talk the talk. The class burst into laughter. From that day on his nick name was "Talking". Another student who was a close friend of his came to the front of the class and worked the problem. I was surprised that his nick became "Walking". Their nick names stuck. To this day they are known as Walking and Talking.

Having spent almost a whole quarter on the water drop-penny experiment, I tried to force the issue to an end by drawing a line in the sand, demanding that a final report on the project be due in one week. The directions for writing the report required that they tell what they were attempting to do, what they did, how they did it, the results they obtained and compile a summary off their results and a data table. After receiving a few draft copies of reports, I distributed a second report writing guide-Appendix VI and a grading rubric. In most cases, what I received was a shell of what I should have received. Most students rewrote what I had asked them to do using my words. Some students outlined what the report should contain and attached an unreadable data table. Some students had rewritten my hand out example explaining how the experiment should work with examples of student grades, added their name and turned that in as their LAB REPORT. Some used the same numbers as if the dummy

grades in the improvised data that I had given them in my hand out and called the data water drops. A few had used a copying machine to copy my handout, added their name and turned it in as their work. Their actions were as if they did not think I would read the report and would place a grade on the report, maybe based on some mythical factor—maybe neatness. It was obvious they had been conditioned to believe that such deceptive work was acceptable with manyb teachers. They were definitely accustomed to and acclimated to low expectations.

Discipline within the whole school was out of hand. There were fights almost every day; fires in the lavatories, and teacher's cars were vandalized. Class cutting and hall roaming was the favorite pass time. I was surprised to learn that, somehow, my car was spared. Some teachers, including myself, took great pride and were elated when their car was spared. We all credited their great relationship with students. Gang activity was rapid.

It is interesting to note that the local police department held a seminar on gang activity for teachers. It included the identification of gang tags and superficial rational of why the gangs formed and why students joined. Two elements of the rational for belonging to a gang stood out to me. I was surprised at how extensive and organized the gang activities were. Deep down within me, I felt the gangs formed as organized crime activity, but the police emphasized that they formed for the protection and companionship that the gangs afforded its members. Some of the gangs were acceptable to the police but they watched all the gangs vary closely for criminal activity. I also felt the sexual initiations, rigidity of their rules and unfettered devotions were part of powerful controlling personalities

MY EGO

and the dogmatic control of its members. I also felt the police had acquiesced a little too much to the gangs. Their tags and graffiti were all over the city and in our school. Their philosophy appeared to be to control and watch the gangs until crimes were committed. Somehow, I felt they should not even exist within the schools but felt powerless to prevent it.

I was surprised to learn that most of the fights were power or prestige related. The game of chicken was a major cause of fights. The game required that when two students met in the hall or on stairs one must yield to the other or a fight would start. Gang activity was growing.

Mid quarter grades had been sent out and I must admit that I had leaned a bit heavily on the students, mostly because of a lack of follow through on check points (status reports), and quiz grades. Deep within my heart I knew that the students did not deserve better grades, yet, I felt deep remorse for them and felt that with a little additional maturity they would turn their lives around.

After the grades went out, the stuff really began to hit the fan. I began to receive nasty notes, most written by students with their parents named signed by the student. I also received a few overt threats. One student had photo copied a note from a friend's parent, signed his own parent's name and passed it to me as if was from his own parent. Then I received a message from the principle that he wanted to discuss a student's grade with me. The student was Kooky.

I was surprised to learn that Kooky's mother was president of the PTA. A conference had been set up between her, the principle and me. As I walked into the principal's office she was seated in a lounge chair arranged somewhat like a living room but suitable for an informal conference. She was as beautiful as ever wearing a mid-length black skirt. Somehow my eyes went directly to her legs and I sensed that she knew it. I was embarrassed at thinking that she would somehow uncross her legs.

I walked forwarded and greeted her with a handshake which she returned and said" Still cannot teach, huh? And there was that smile.

After reminiscing about my teaching, her days as my student and reviewing some of Kooky's work, she became somewhat conciliatory, yet direct and more polished than I had expected. She told me that she wanted her daughter to go to Harvard and needed my help. The principle's facial expression let out a chuckle which was so funny I had to bite my lip to not show what I knew he was thinking. My heart began to pound when she said, "How about lunch soon?" The principle's face let out another hidden chuckle. I said, "Sure, why not"? I felt a warm feeling below my stomach. Caution took over my rational being and I thought that I had better be careful. But, being manipulated may not be that bad, I thought.

SOCIETY, TEACHERS AND THE STUDENT

After school my mind wandered back to my research mode. Could it be that the needs of our students and their quest for self-actualization have breed students that are dominating, manipulating, and selfish, dishonest, greedy, intimating and a host of other traits showing neurotic tendencies, somewhat as suggested by Horney, and this has led to massive disruption and out of control schools? One has to wonder when and how did this get started. These trends, as other characteristics noted at other schools appear to have developed gradually but were accelerating at an exponential rate and are engulfing other factions of our society.

Looking at the publicized mentality of our present day business and political world shows that greed also fits the trend. When one looks at the need for success in the business world, there is a direct correlation with the need for more self-actualization and the resulting traits imparted to students pand to the business world. I will hesitate before I say that the adult world suffers from the exact neurosis but it is acknowledged that when the needs of the business leaders and politicians are not met, neurosis can develop. I also realized that the business leaders of today were the students of yesteryear. In the popular movie "Wall Street" Michael Douglas coined the phrase "Greed is good" suggesting that everything is fair that gets results. Maybe this was the beginning of a mentality that has engulfed our society. One only need to look at the number of high tech crimes based on greed, manipulations, fraud, domination, lies and other disruptive characteristics. There is a direct correlation with what we are experiencing in our schools. The major difference is that, in our schools, the actions by students seeking self-actualization are less sophisticated. Consider the following.

1. Leading presidential candidate appoints virtually unknown as his running mate. This has to be an attempt at a manipulation of sorts.
2. Finance leaders pay out lucrative bonuses after receiving governmental payout funds. Manipulation, greed and an expression of dominance were factors.

3. Governor denies trying to sell senate seat after government produces tapes as evidence. Greed, pride and a feeling of entitlement were evident.
4. Auto leaders report to congressional hearing on bailout in private jets. A feeling of entitlement was exhibited.
5. President goes to war over weapons of mass destruction after being advised that the weapons do not exist. No Comment but I feel revenge and a restitution of pride might be a factor.
6. President has an illicit sex affair and confesses to the nation that he did it because he could.
7. Presidential candidate reported that she was dodging sniper fire when in fact she was not.
8. Weapons supplied to Mexican drug cartel by American business runs rampart.
9. Bank foreclosures halted-blames faulty paper. Bank official signed forecloses without reading them.
10. Official goes to jail for 50 billion dollar Ponzi scheme.
11. News commentators on television distort and manipulate data for political reasons and openly disrespect the president.

I do not want to, but I could add Kooky's panty episodes and any number of student actions to this list because there is a direct correlation with what I am thinking. I originally felt the episodes were a childish attempt at recognition. My cynical mind suggested to me something more devious was involved—maybe she was a prostitute, turning fast tricks whenever she got the opportunity. I questioned why I did not want to believe this. My pornographic mind produced all sorts of images which I tried to erase.

One could rationalize the reported incidents as trivia caused by inaccurate reporting by the press, or minor mistakes in judgment, or they are psychotically derived or any number of other excuses or factors. But in each of the above cases, the reported propitiator would be expected to exhibit the highest level of conduct, integrity and business consistent with good rational and moral law or just plain old morality. Each involves a thought process that resulted in an action. It was hopefully believed that a form of neurosis had caused the actions. I thought of greed and selfness and of the parable of the man who did like his shoes.

"The man did not like his shoes. He did not like the way they looked, his feet hurt after walking a distance, and they took too long to dry when they were wet. He was totally disgusted with the shoes until he came across a man who had no feet. He was now so elated that he had shoes and liked the feeling he derived when he compared himself with the man with no feet that he begin to chop off the feet of other men so that he could enjoy more of the elation he felt when he saw men with no feet" (Unknown origin).

Embedded in this parable is another concept related to self-actualization. "True self-actualization should only be obtained from within oneself and never through the demise of another.

Could Karen Horney be correct? Was I looking at a wide spread epidemic of neurotic behavior? I turned on the television. Indeed, neurotic behavior was everywhere. I begin to think seriously about our schools and our society. I begin to get a believable picture of how neurosis could easily develop in children, continue into their adulthood and become ingrained into our society shaping our beliefs and behavior towards each other. This type rational began to weigh more heavily on my mind and I was beginning to believe it more and more each day, The fights and other disruptions, the high dropout rates, increased teen pregnancies, openly defiant, hostile and disrespectful students, finagling students, increased crime, low test scores; all this coupled with what was happening with our society in general was correlating into something that was getting hard to handle. On the adult side, there were increased divorce rates, road rage, increased domestic violence, violent and drug related crimes, and increases in racial turmoil. There was a definite correlation between adults and the student's activity.

Was Kooky's episode with the panties caused by societal creep? I thought of the day when actors on TV would not kiss on the lips and for a man and woman to appear in bed together was unheard of. Now sex on TV and in the movies is common. Was Kooky in search of self-actualization and this was the method she chose to seek recognition? Although kooky was weighing heavily on my mind, I could not completely reconcile her actions.

These children also form ideas of how their success relates to other people—the competitiveness and a meaning of success and all the related interactions that enhance success and failure. Once a student starts school his interaction with more diverse people increases tremendously and his needs, which are related to the new interactions, change and so must his coping strategies change. The road to success becomes more complex. How he deals with deprived self-actualization becomes of uttermost importance and is not as smooth regardless of the background of the student. Thus, our trend and problems with learning are not just restricted to the down trotted but is extended to the affluent who must also compete in a society bent on their destruction at the hands of competitive greed. The down trotted are exposed to a double whammy.

Disruptive behavior in our schools is worst in the middle schools where students are less mature and their mental processes are more susceptible to manipulation by unfulfilled and newer needs. The reactions to their needs are more intense and more spontaneous and therefore more disruptive to the teachers.

Likewise, our inner cities and urban areas are frothed with deprived self-actualizations. Survival is more competitive, and life is more of a struggle, especially for people with lower incomes when compared with our suburban areas. Therefore if deprived self-actualization is a strong factor, there is little wonder why discipline is more of a problem in these schools, their test scores are lower and the students are more difficult to teach.

I considered the following stats published in Ed Week by Elena Aguilar.

- Nine out of 10 teachers in the United States are white.
- Four out of every 10 students are not white.
- Some 40 percent of public schools have no teachers of color.
- In diverse classrooms, issues of race and culture masquerade behind differences in learning and communication styles, attitudes, interests, behavior, and much more.
- It is the teacher's responsibility to bridge this cultural chasm. We cannot eliminate the differences but we can learn to communicate effectively and deal with each other. It Maters that 90 percent of teachers are white. Let's accept

this notion and acknowledge that race is an uncomfortable issue to deal with, mostly because our society has placed such emphasis on racial perceptions. But I am not sure that race matters in the same context that is commonly purported—that there is a difference in learning styles between races, cultures, religions, economic backgrounds, neighborhoods, and any other factors that may be conjured up, that concerns what is purported as race.

I had also learned a valuable lesson about forming opinions about students, their learning habits and how learning is strongly related to life's experiences. This incident suggests that we should reevaluate how we test learning and attempt to better alien student learning with, for lack of a better term, with learning processes. The popular recommendation that teachers must get to know their students because they cannot teach a student they do not know is a myth, I thought. Sometimes when the teacher feels they know students, especially minority students, the perception is based on some poorly understood, yet widely publicized, concept of that minority group as a whole. The reality is that there is a greater difference in personalities, and preferred learning styles within any racial group than there is between the groups. Often the perceived knowledge that teachers have been taught or have learned about the races is used in a negative punitive manor. For example, often when there is some disagreement or minor dispute the eye concept is played and the person gets in the face of the minority and glairs into his eyes until the minority looks away. When it is perceived that the person resents the eye contact, which is usually the case with students, the glare is sometimes intended and, more importantly perceived by the student as a punitive gesturer. It appears as if every white person is schooled in this concept and uses it to their advantage at their leisure.

Another vivid recall I have is that of a student, recently from West Africa, who I considered one of my worst chemistry students because I felt he had zero technical perception. While teaching a class on air and pressure and demonstrating the effect of pressure on liquids, he said let me show you something. He picked up an Erlenmeyer flask, filled it with about an inch from the bottom with water. He slapped an open palm down on the open end of the flask. The bottom of the flask fell out, breaking in an almost perfect circle. As a teacher, I realized the concept immediately but had never thought of it in such dramatic fashion. I had also learned a new lesson about water and air pressure and about the biased judgment of students that teachers have about students they think they know. The technical perception displayed by his demonstration was outstanding. It showed that he toughly understood how force acted on liquids. I asked the student where had learned how to do the trick. He said that he did not know but eventually relate it to fishing with dynamite in his native country. At first, he was reluctant to discuss fishing with explosives as it is outlawed in his country.

When a teacher attempts to learn the habits of a group of students and has 183 students, the individual habits involved and the number of habits to be effectively learned increases exponentially. The amount of time and money spent trying to teach teachers about the learning styles and habits of different ethnic groups have been for nothing and the reported results show it. Because of the diversity within each ethnic group, the possibility of a missed diagnosis increases dramatically. Most

ERLENMEYER FLASK

recent reports show that the gap in performance between racial groups is widening. But is this really true? Minority groups are still reported to lag behind in academic performances. But sub groups within the minorities are shown to excel. Yet research reports expounding the inferiority of minority groups as a whole entity keep rolling off the presses. Could it be because such reports are good fodder for our expanding dogmatic society? When the data on all groups is combined, do other sub groups emerge as significant? Such groups might be economic categories where sharp breaks occur as poverty levels increase. The real problem is that as the poverty groups are identified the dogmatic mentality turns to something resembling hate, especially when it is not meeting the needs of the purveyor or is based on some ego trip. Hate groups are reservoirs for the dogmatic mentality. The dogmatic mentality often results with an astounding "I told you so". I do not intend to re-write the statistical analysis book, but I question the dogma of our researchers for not looking past the obvious and our politicians for not taking appropriate action in this regard and teachers for believing the hype about racial differences.

I can recall a parent teacher conference with both parents of a flunking student. The students augment was a common one. He claimed to be a kinesthetic type learner and needed more hands on type teaching. My reply, and his father agreed but his mother never did, was that he should learn any way he could and must practice all types of learning, even though some learning might be a little more painful for him. My augment is that regardless of how hard we try, we will never master the inner thoughts and requirements to teach all 183 students. Likewise, teachers must teach the best way they can and always remember that experience is golden. Another point is that students must want to learn and put forth real effort to learn. They must be taught that mastery of the subject matter is their responsibility and they should never hide behind the teacher's responsibility to teach them. Open and real communications between student and teacher can help with understanding of complex subject matter without going into deep theoretical analysis of personality.

My memory goes back further to the penny-water drop experiment. When I attempted to expand the lesson to include surface and interfacial tensions, and onto capillary action, the best correlation with the phenomena of absorption suggesting that students understood the lesson was absorption by a sanitary napkin. I was puzzled by the student's correlation. Then I realized that a students learning is closely related to their life's experiences. Several classes ago, I had used cotton to demonstrate absorption.

My thoughts immediately returned to the Kooky and her no pantie antics. Could it have been that, in her search for unfulfilled self-actualization, that this was the best or perhaps only cooping strategy she knew that would bring her instant recognition? Could her actions be related to the motivation driving similar antics of a flasher? A flasher's motivation is obviously related to a quest for recognition or self-actualization. Now, I am seriously questioning my own logic, asking whether I am experiencing more of the funny stuff originating from the Hood where coping strategies are based on whatever is available. My analytical mind tells me I should see more of it from the hood or maybe it appears in a different form when it originates from a different source, or maybe it is indeed based on is based on different life experiences.

I was getting to know Tray fairly well, I thought—a student somewhat like myself at that age. He would stop by from time to time just to talk.

We would hold lengthy one on one conversation at least once per week. One day the conversation turned to the experience in the army. Tray asked if I had ever killed someone and I replied maybe. The student became excited and passionately asked if I had ever got a "Head Shot". Searching for something to say that would not be a lie; I asked if it really mattered. The student asked again with double passion "Did you"?

My first inclination was that Tray was or had become some sort of morbid crackpot and wanted me to join him in gloating over an act of morbid desiccation. This did not change my impression of this favorite student. I really felt he was a good level headed student. Later, and after further investigation, I mistakenly concluded that Tray felt locked in the ghetto and his only way out was thru the military. He really liked the army but had a morbid fear of combat. My original analysis had changed my impression of him, until later I found that the real problem was that he had just watched a combat movie. Based on my experience in the military, Tray and his questions were then normal. I felt really ashamed and thought of the real challenge of really getting to know 183 high school students per year, each with their own fairly well formed perceptions of life. Students below 7th grade are forming their perception of life and present a different subject.

Was Kooky and Snow Flake really gay or were their actions spurred by some other mechanism such as teen sexual confusion interacting with their emotions. Was Woody, who stole a half pound of pastrami and tried to bribe me with it really a crook or was it that his life experiences led him to believe that give in order to get is a normal way of life. And, I must point out that wrong should always be pointed out and never condoned with students, regardless of how sympathetic you might feel about their actions.

My more potent point is that children from the hood, by virtue of their limited life experiences, their unusual coping strategies posed by unfulfilled self-actualizations, may appear as children with limited intellect, but may be highly perceptive about certain other things.

The most important lesson I have learned relates teacher to student as well as student to teacher and is as simple as eating ice cream. The relationship must be based on mutual respect for each other and exhibit a firm understanding of each other's roll in the relationship. The teacher's job is to teach and the student's job is to learn. And, most teachers do not realize that part of their job is to teach the student how to learn and above all that the students must learn to teach themselves. Other than that, the teacher must never teach the student what they cannot learn or by any means restrict the student's learning based on some unfounded opinion about what they cannot learn. They must teach them to develop the joy of learning. And at the high school level, they must increase their exposure to life's experiences and expectations and the proper relationship to each other. In the teaching of any lesson or subject, the teacher must attempt to maximize the student's life experience on the subject. In other words get the student to go into as much depth on the issue as is possible and guide them into maximum exploration.

I agree that teachers should be evaluated. But extreme care is advised. Students are smarter than most people realize. They are also conniving, vindictive and sometimes angry. Our

49

society has taught this to our students. They go into action the moment an administrator walks into a classroom and are as engaging as they want to be. The administrator who feels smart enough to see through the students is sadly mistaken. Even multiple visits cannot solve this problem, and it should be realized that the teacher, regardless of his skill cannot teach or display his wares when the students do not want him to do so.

These contentions point to the basic problem with school reform, discipline or the lack of it. And, it makes little difference whether the students are good, bad, smart or dumb, pretty of ugly; they enjoy the power they have over teachers. We have given this and taught it to them to them. Students are engaged when it is easy and when they easily experience the elation of success. The students have taught us to believe that they learn when they are experiencing happiness. And, believe me they know how to fake happy and sad. Let's realize the basic problem—the students we have created.

I had always considered myself an excellent checker player. With most opponents, I could reverse the board after they had lost all but two men and still win the match. I taught one of my perceived poorer students how to play checkers and after six months he was better than me. I later found that he had been practicing with everybody he could find. He had learned to love checkers. At first I rationalized that he loved checkers because he could beat almost every one he played. I later found that he also loved to teach checkers. His skill at checkers was born from within himself, not by cheating or finagling his opponents. He also learned chess and formed a checker-chess-club that met several days per week after school. I wondered. Does it take greater intelligence to play checkers or learn chemistry or does it really depend on what the student is interested in?

At the moment my thinking concentrated on teachers and their relationship to the diversity of their students.

Being a minority myself, my thoughts spearheaded to such words and thoughts that I feel may be barriers to learning—such as disrespect, unfairness, and preconceived opinions, fear of oppression, domination, unfair competition, invisibility. These are all factors that we as a dogmatic society may exert on our students and on each other, sometimes not realizing it. I thought to myself as a chemist, dam those interactions—things that act one way when acted upon alone but differently when combined with other variables. Trying to be objective in my thoughts, I wondered how any parent or average citizen subjected to an identical situation as a minority student in a hostile class room would react. Or, how would a young minority chemist entering into a new job where most of his colleagues felt him strange and some felt he did not belong, was not qualified, or even feared him. How much of this resulting frustration would he take home and implant in his children? Deprived self-actualization, what effect does it have on what we are seeing in our schools? What can teachers do about it?

I was reminded of a prayer someone sent to me.
"Dear Lord: We have lost our spiritual equilibrium and reversed our values
We have exploited the poor and called it the lottery.
We have rewarded laziness and called it welfare.
We have killed our unborn and called it choice.

We have shot abortionists and called it justifiable...
We have neglected to discipline our children and called it building self-esteem.
We have abused power and called it politics.
We have coveted our neighbor's possessions and called it ambition.
We have polluted the air with profanity and pornography and called it freedom of expression.
We have ridiculed the time-honored values of our forefathers and called it enlightenment.
We have bombed our friends and called it liberation
Search us, Oh, God, and know our hearts today; cleanse us from every sin and set us free.
Amen!

Some of the points exhibited in the prayer are debatable but the prayer connotes our drift towards a dogmatic society.

Teachers must feel the pain of their students—all students. They must rid their selves of all the stereotype beliefs about ethnic groups, both poor and wealthy, then decide that all students will be treated the same. <u>The overall student requirement for special teaching skills by a teacher is much more diverse between individuals than you will find between any ethnic or religious group, between rich or poor students.</u> Teachers must be sensitive to the fact that the students may enter their class with all the barriers to learning there is. Remember that, for most minority students, an important barrier to learning is a fear that the teacher may have a preconceived idea of them especially those that see the pussy cat in the mirror. If the teacher plays to that perception, other students will know it and the sparrow of mistrust becomes even more pervasive. Ego is the king of sensitivities. Next is the belief in the possibilities that they will not be successful.

Most minority students will project that they see a lion in the mirror, but many will actually see a pussy cat in the mirror. As students enter your class, most will have experienced every type of emotional degradation you as a teacher can imagine. They are extremely astute at detecting any and all types of biases, both real and imaginary. Once, the student has overcome these obstacles, they are ready to start what they perceive as the pain of learning. In spite of all this, teachers should never ever pamper students in their quest to learn, mostly because the results are too habit forming with students. An occasional expressions of sympathy shows concern but pampering is a no-no, and expectations must drive student motivations.

Student disruptions are learned traits—habits that we have bred into the students by not recognizing their quest for self-actualization. The lack of self-actualization has caused deep seated neurotic traits. The real challenge is to determine what should be done or what is the best method of correction for the problems RELATED TO STUDENTS WANTING TO LEARN. How do we correct the problem of disruptive students or maybe we should agree that the bigger problem is that our whole society is experiencing neurotic traits and direct the real challenge at the whole society. Then the question becomes how do we correct it all? What is the best way to change what is perceived to be human nature or human behavior?

Through the eyes of a research scientist, one would agree that human behavior is engulfed with interacting and almost unidentifiable variables, each yielding distantly different outcomes. This suggests that these many variables and the problems poised, together, are unsolvable. But most scientists do not believe this. On the surface, the approach to solving these type problems is to lump the

variables together and try to move the whole pile, looking at results as a whole entity, rather than the undefined inter related individual variables.

As my school year progressed, I began to learn better what I will call the teacher lesson and lessons about people in general—How grownups correlated with the students I was teaching. Going back to my undergraduate days I can recall one of my professors in the school of education advising us that a teacher who does not understand people was not worth a dam.

Was Hillary Clinton who lied twice on national TV about sniper fire a pathological liar? Was Bernie Madoff, the financier who was convicted of stealing billions of dollars really a crook? And, how about the news commentators who would distort, and misquote news items in attempts to manipulate public opinion? Were these news correspondents motivated by personal or political gain or themselves manipulated by other co-operate interties with more complex yet distorted motives? Are the rapid increases in societal crimes, all characterized by greed, manipulations, pride, deprived self-actualizations, neurotic comparisons, all part of our normal society? In each case the evidence says yes to all this? We as a society will accept some of these and rationalize others. For children, we tend to accept traits such as moodiness, lack of impulse control, a need for instant gratification, addictive behavior, and codependence, manipulative character, self-centered—inappropriate and uncontrollable outburst of anger, depression and irritability and other manifestations of distorted personalities. One thing for sure is that these and many other negative traits are increasing at an abnormal rate for students, politicians, and many other citizens.

I have begun to wonder if we are victims of a societal creep, where over time, our basic beliefs about our relations to each other are also changing: where we no longer believe that hard work is the key to success but rather conniving manipulations leading to domination over each other is the key to success. Wow! Have I cracked and turned into a crazy paranoid?

My thoughts turned to a political philosophy of war. Could we as a nation with super powers gain influence over a corrupt and somewhat undeveloped nation with humanitarian gestures such as improving their education and way of life or must we first gain domination over the corruption with military might. My estimate is that 25 years ago our nation would vote 75 percent for the humanitarian approach but my estimate is that now only 50 percent would favor the humanitarian approach. Such a change in philosophy correlates well with what we are now experiencing in our societal relationships, and what I call a societal creep towards a dogmatic way of life. Could it be that our present way of life with its demands for social, monetary and other acceptance criteria have over taxed our psyche leading to a neurotic creep into a dogmatic way of life that is pervasive? And, is this dogmatic way of life showing itself, first and more dramatically, in our schools, more so in our inner-city schools where life is tougher and the struggle by blacks and other minorities are more prominent?

This type thinking was a little too much, even for my psyche, I finally fell asleep about 3:00AM I woke up about 6:00AM and got ready to face another day of teaching but with my ideas falling into place. I could see correlations within the complex matrices of personalities and actions.

It is interesting to note that I taught High Pockets how to balance chemical equations and he was so proud that he taught it to the whole track and basketball teams. Woody learned how to calculate the yield of a chemical reaction from any amount of starting materials: even without ever really running a chemical reaction. The pride derived from their accomplishments was obvious. From these accomplishments, I surmised that these students could learn and wanted to learn. My thoughts returned to why they weren't learning.

When discussing student performance with other teachers, a multitude of opinions of why the students are not learning developed rapidly.

Snowflake became pregnant and a few years later came by to see me with a beautiful baby boy. She put the baby down and as he crawled across the floor, I thought "Dam, he reminded me of a giraffe". His arms were long and held his head high in relation to the rest of his body. I shouted without really thinking "Slinky". She smiled and replied "Yes, we are married and he is playing basketball in Europe and hopes to be in the NBA next year". She spoke with such pride of their accomplishments that I, myself, was wreaked with pride. She informed me that Kooky did not make Harvard but was admitted to a medical technology program in Kansas. I had also known her mother's pride. Snowflake also informed me that no one knows where Woody was except that he left town to work at a meat packing place somewhere in the South. High Pockets was a wide receiver on a Canadian football team.

Tray, the student I nurtured, and tried to impart my own virtues, was accepted into a military academy prep school. I felt that with earlier help, he would have been admitted directly into a military academy. As I could have guested, Talking was working his way through a pre-law curriculum at a state university and Walking had graduated from a tech school and was working in an electrician's apprentice.

Not all was so rosy. Joey, the student whose mother thought he was servicing his English teacher was nabbed as the getaway driver in a jewelry store heist. He had sent me a message that he had messes up big time and was sorry. I wished I had taught him to be sorry for himself and to be more responsible for himself but, I guessed, I had not taught him enough even though I considered him as potentially a good student. Perhaps the demons of ambition had overtaken him before he could learn the lesson of pride from within himself.

Expectations, has to be a strong factor with student motivation. Expectations and accomplishments breed pride. Could these be missing factors in the mentality and homes of underprivileged children? What about the school life of these children? If they are factors, could our schools restore these missing factors? The missing expectations, Yes! With pride, only well-defined goals and accomplishments can gain this.

There was no doubt in my mind that most of the students, who many teachers write off as losers, were actually smart enough to be winners. Yet, I sensed that there were correction factors somewhere in their heads that needed addressing. I also sensed that their needs were far beyond the need for number skills or basic math. As I taught them the elementary math skills needed for high school chemistry, they took great pride in learning even the most elementary things. Shame was not a direct factor. But, I wonder how the negative publicity related to the inferiority of minorities really affected my students. The public and school administrators appear to use low test scores to motivate teachers and students and boast their own feelings of superiority. Somehow I felt this is wrong.

The effect of negative publicity on students is tremendous. Can you imagine how it feels to constantly read or hear that minorities score low on every test that is given, or that you are part of a statistic that tell you that you stand a 1 in 4 chance of ending up in jail or not graduating from high school? For many, these messages should be motivators for self-improvement and they are for some. But the constant bombardment with these tit bits takes their toll on the soul and leads to denied self-actualization for far too many.

Would you believe that Christmas holidays were beginning? After about a day of nothing, I sat down and in an almost isolated room. I tried to consolidate what I thought of the problems of teaching. The first problem I noticed and the one that pissed me off the most was that teachers were being hammered by the public, the press and politicians. Students were noticing this also. One told me

"You caught a lot of shit in the newspapers today, didn't you". I never thought of quitting. Here is what I wrote in my solitude.

CHAPTER III

*An **Additional** Word About the Habits of Students*

I had the opportunity to observe a 2 ½ year male for a significant amount of time. This kid was extremely active, would not sit still, was extremely destructive and well on a path where several other observers who were more learned in child phycology than me, felt that he was definitely an ADHD (attention-deficit/hyperactivity disorder) kid. One day, this kid was wailing at the top of his voice in a room full of people, and no one, including his mother could stop him from crying. I walked into the room and asked in a loud voice, "who is that crying'? There was a pause in his crying and he replied "Me", and then started crying again. There was no doubt in my mind that he was crying for attention, and the type of attention he craved was specific, and deliberate.

I continued to observe him in other situations, noting that he was deliberately destructive and often selective with what he destroyed. Usually, he selected the most expensive items which I interpreted as the ones that would get him the most attention. For example, in a room full of people, he selected adults over other children, a knife at a dinner table rather than a spoon to wave and bang on the table with. He announced to his father that he was going to pee on the rug when he could just as well peed on the wood or tile floor. Could his selections have been so deliberate at an age of only 2 ½? My analytical mind tells me that, on statistical basics and based on the observations, yes, they were that deliberate and selective, especially after observing a few other episodes. He painted the keys on a piano, marked up the monitor of a computer and emptied a flower pot on the living room rug. I should have child proofed my home.

I ease-dropped on a conversation between his mother and another woman when she complained that she would sometimes fall asleep only to be awaken by him pounding on her breasts. Again I surmised that his actions were deliberate and directed towards a specific type attention.

The point of all this was that I had begun to believe that this kid, even at the age of 2 ½, was the victim of learned behavior. And, it was unfortunate that he had learned negative behavior. His parents were well educated and successful. Yet, they had fallen prey to a lack of properly directed education on child rearing. For example, in the first case, I feel their kid was a victim of denied self-actualization and had learned to cry to attract attention to his plight—his coping strategy was to cry.

In the second case, his strategy was to be destructive and he had learned that he would get more immediate attention if he destroyed something of value. The third case, I feel, is a little more complicated. Most mothers know that their children should be weaned from the bottle, but most do not know or perhaps never thought about weaning their kid from the breast to the bottle. Neither did my wife and I. Fortunately, our kids were started on breast in combination with the bottle. Weaning was by accident more natural.

The number of ADHD students in our schools is rapidly increasing and so is the number of students diagnosed as requiring special needs. The cost of educating these students is also increasing rapidly. Our educational researchers have blamed parental influence, drugs, poverty, and a host of other things. Traditionally, our schools will pass these problems on as something we must have and live with. We have hired additional school psychologist and councilors rather than thinking outside the box, determining the cause, and eliminating the cause of the rapid increase within the school junta. Here, I blame educational researchers and teachers more so than anyone else for not attacking the problem more methodically. Maybe our economic interest related to the monetary value of an increase in the number of ADHD kids was a factor for our deficient research into the causes area was a factor.

I do not profess to be learned in child phycology. But as a research chemist, I am trained to think outside the box and to look for the unusual. Can 2 ½ year old children have developed such learned mentality to create an increase in ADHD students in our schools as is suggested by the observations of this 2 ½ old child.? Could better education of the parents prevent the problems they were experiencing? Could better educating our students have produced better mothers and fathers? Is the increase in ADHD students the result of improper diagnoses? Is ADHD more of a learn trait rather than a medical condition that should be treated with drugs? What happened to "home economics, or better yet, home and family life science classes which were taught in some schools, then discontinued? To mention the advocacy of uniform curriculums at this junction may seem out of place. Therefore I shall only mention that it is counterproductive to creative thinking—one of the areas that are plaguing the teaching profession. Such is counterproductive for our high schools and our teacher prep institutions.

I also feel that medical research, more specifically, in areas of behavior research have dropped the ball and opted for treatment rather than causes and cures. These observations also suggest that behavior problems start at ages well below what is normally considered by parents.

CHAPTER IV

Present Day Teachers

For the most part teachers are the unsung heroes of most school systems. Yet they are considered by popular belief, to be the purveyors of most of the problems with schools. Administrators and teacher educators express the need for more and better teacher training, elimination of teacher unions, reduced class size, better pedagogy, the need for a more uniform curriculum, problems with special education, better classroom management, better school atmosphere—and the list goes on to, occasionally, includes a need for better school management. But when teachers and their problems are looked at with a critical scientific eye a different view of their problems and needs emerge with several new theories.

One thing for sure, the student song of boring teachers is one that should be erased and never uttered again. Almost any teacher trying to teach will be boring to some students and heroes to others. Boring is a dramatic excuse, created by students, to compensate for the pain of learning and their determination to not learn. It has led teachers to deviate from their natural methods of teaching and spend time, money and an enormous amount of energy at entertaining students. Some students will like the teacher for whatever the reason. Thus, in the eyes of some, there are good and bad teachers. This contention, I thought, was the beginning of the big debate on teacher proficiency but does not excuse teachers from any and all criticism.

Once the frustrations of trying to teach sets in, most present day teachers, especially of intercity students, appear to be resolved that the teaching of the defiant students was impossible. These theories suggest that teachers are the victims rather than the culprits. To their dismay, teachers have fallen prey to the apparent characteristics exhibited by the children and the inability of society to make the appropriate adjustments. Teacher unions, trade organization, and administrators have been of little or no help to the teachers because the prevailing theories and thus, most of their efforts at helping the teachers have been bases on invalid causes and the demons of teacher bashing. Teachers are their own best critics. There conversations only need a keen ear and analysis of their complaints.

Following are excerpts of the present day teacher's conversations about teaching.

1. Sometimes I fear that we will lose faith—in ourselves and our children. Many teachers find their classes harder, their children demonstrating fewer academic and social skills. In my school, too, the challenges can be daunting. More than ever we need to feel the courage and hope of our professions. We need the time and stamina to problem-solve, to search in our own midst for effective strategies and to collaborate.
2. Classes had been dismissed for lunch and the hallway was alive with kids going into lockers, heading for rest

rooms, and meeting friends...I saw Patricia and James playfully arguing. Suddenly, with the grace of a dancer, Patricia's leg shot out and kicked a laughing James with a sideswipe worthy of Jean-Claude Van Dame

3. My biggest stress has to do with the issues that kids come to school with that are so difficult to identify. I've had these children for two months almost [this school year] and there are still issues that hold up their educational process. I talk to parents but still can't get the children to attend to the task given. It's not an academic problem, it's a social problem.
   Getting kids to open up; developing the skills needed to create independent problem-solvers; developing respect among students; and getting kids to take responsibility for their own learning. Those are the sorts of problems teachers face every day. Big problems—problems without simple answers.

4. Lessons Right now my biggest issue is behavior management, getting control of the class to get across effectively. When you have a class size that is pretty much capacity, at 32 kids, the room is filled, and you never have everyone on task and focused.

5. It seems that over the years my students have become increasingly non-verbal and passive...They need to be prodded to express themselves in a class discussion or to share something about themselves. When they do speak, they offer only the required amount of information

6. Differentiating instructions so that the needs and learning styles of all students are met is a constant source of stress. The "No Child Left Behind" motto is one that teachers take very seriously, but constantly struggle with how to accomplish the goal.

7. This is my 16th year teaching secondary English, and what seems to be wearing me down is the paper load. The multiple-choice and short-answer questions are relatively manageable, but the essays and research projects are a burden. They consume three to four hours of each Saturday morning, and as happy as I am to wake up to a day without bells, the stack of essays [to grade] sits like a weight on my spirits. Occasionally I conduct peer-editing and self-editing lessons, but still have not found a way to significantly reduce the long hours of

8. For the modern educator, there is no greater stress than wanting to succeed admirably at an important task and being systematically denied the resources to do so, but that is precisely the fate awaiting most who undertake the job of teaching. To paraphrase the old real estate adage, the three secrets of effective teaching are: time, time and time. The requirements for presenting excellent instruction are: time to plan effective lessons, time to present those lessons and, finally, time to assess whether learning has taken place. All three are absolutely essential to improving student achievement.

9. Today, however, good teaching transpires mostly where teachers donate innumerable hours of non-compensated time to the schools for the purposes of planning and assessment... Teachers in your typical school are in front of children for 275 minutes a day, and if they are fortunate, they have a paltry 45 minutes to plan their lessons. The remainder of a teacher's requisite planning must be performed outside the seven-hours.

10. My biggest professional stress is trying to motivate students to learn when they don't have any motivation coming in. A lot of kids have not hooked into the fact that learning is important...

The above excerpts characterize our present day teachers who love teaching and love their jobs but are losing it. Their problems are interactive. The frustrations caused by neurotic, disgruntled students coupled with the loud voices of disgruntled parents and pushy administrators are daunting. Disgruntled parents often turn to administrators for help when problem arises. The administrators often do not analyze these problems but will approach the teacher, often with disdain leading to more frustrated teachers. Once the frustrations of trying to teach sets in, most present day teachers, especially of intercity students appear to be resolved that the teaching of the defiant students is impossible and most stop effective teaching.

These theories and the teachers themselves are easy targets of prey for critics as well as researchers. The lack of classroom management skills is the favorite target used by first echelon administrators who are usually responsible for discipline matters. The teachers, especially the more experienced ones become resolved that the best way to handle defiant student behavior is through appeasement. They have become very astute at alleviating rowdy and defiant student's problems using day to day remedies. Their remedies are time consuming at the expense of real academics and offer little or no effort towards improving student performance. The main goal of most intercity teachers is to get through the day.

On the other hand, students will observe the teacher, analyze and learn the habits of teachers with the skill of a seasoned research scientist and go into action with their own remedies, often at the expense of the teacher. There are far too many teachers who really like their jobs as teachers. But, because of the defiant rowdy and unmotivated students, they are finding their job frustrating if not impossible. Administrators tend to join with the pacifying teachers and do not require that they teach. They require only that the teachers keep order.

Students will observe the teacher, analyze and learn the habits of teachers with the skill of a seasoned research scientist and go into action with their own remedies, often at the expense of the teacher.

Teachers mollify the students with trivia work that the student can successfully do with little or no effort. This seems to pacify the students and they are happy with the apparent self-actualization that the easy work affords. Another approach is to simply entertain the students. Chemistry classes are always boring unless something burns. Math classes, because of their requirement for critical thinking, are just as bad for the students. Present day pedagogy dictates an interest approach at the start of each class. This technique appeared to serve the teachers well and some teachers would extent the interest approach, as entertainment, for the whole period. The student's voice expressing boredom and frustration with teaching is loud and clear.

Quiet students are often allowed to sit in the rear of the class and doodle as long as they do not disturb the class. Students learn quickly that this and a smile will please the teacher and they will pass the class.

I am still trying to analyze a documentary on education presented by MSNBC which depicted a fight between two girls in a 4th or 5th grade class. The girl on the winning side of the fight was about twice the size of the other girl and appeared to have started the fight. First, I question whether the parents of either child gave permission to air their children in such a vicious fight. Except for depicting the trials and tribulations of teaching, there was no other mention of the fight with in the documentary. Second there was a seen of students lined up as if they were waiting for something and the teacher was voicing displeasure of the students. In all the seams, the students appeared to be minorities. Most of the students in the depictions appeared to show strong nonverbal mannerisms of resentment. In these days of racial strife, i thought the television stations should reframe from depicting races in such negative light unless they are making specific reference to what they are depicting.

The problems of teachers are directly related to failing schools. Maybe we should call these "the practices of teachers" rather than "the problems of teacher". They raise the question, "What comes first, the chicken or the egg". Negative practices by teachers certainly do not improve the situations of poor student performance but it is not the true cause. The need for and the struggle for students to obtain self-actualization appears to be a main reason for defiant students, classroom management problems, low test scores, teacher frustration, high droop out rates(see appendix #), and a whole host of other problems related to the dilemma of poor performing schools. Educating teachers on the neurotic needs of students would, without a doubt help the situation but is not a total solution or guarantee to solve all the problems. Physiology and the neurotic needs of students is not a major item in the curriculum for teacher education, at least not in the form that it should be.

As I reviewed what I had written it all made sense to me. Our education system is one big interacting agglomcration of mess factors and it makes little sense to point fingers or try to determine how it all got started—by bad students, genetically inferior students, lack of student motivation, bad teachers, lousy administrators /poor managers, lousy parents, poorly funded education, poor teacher preparation and last but not least—politicians. All of these are factors in the mess and dooms day is just around the corner. In thinking about a solution, I cannot help but reflect on my own background—a poor black kid who somehow got out of the hood and manage to mingle with the rich and famous, the good, bad, ugly acting, the beautiful and the righteous. And, I have concluded that there is not a spoonful of difference in learning ability between any of us except for life's experiences and the interaction some people call luck and others may call divine interventions. Luck and divine intervention, I will not touch.

My analytical mind again kicked into high gear and I thought, the best and most efficient way to interact with life's experiences or to optimize life' experiences, for the best possible effect, is through education. Here I thought "Dame Teachers". THEY COULD HAVE PREVENTED THE MESS WITH A LITTLE FORETHOUGHT.

Teachers have unfettered access to students for 12 of their formative years and for more effective hours per day than most working parents. If 10 percent of the teachers are bad teachers, 90% are good teachers and most are at least certified. Could we have more than 10 percent bad teacher? I don't think so. But, regardless, for the most part, I cannot think of any other entity that is in a better position to have affected or should have affected our way of life than teachers. And they have done what I considered an excellent job until lately—until the big interacting agglomeration of mess factors set in on our society. History suggests that we formed a more perfect union, and became the most desirable nation on earth, through education, all after the exertion of our military might. Far too many people forget that our military might was built through education. Thus, the egg came before the chicken. My contention is that if teachers had exerted the proper influence on students, the present situation leading to our demise, should not have developed. Dam, I thought? What Happened? Now, I have begun to point fingers and it is looking in the direction of the teachers—for the cause and, hopefully, the solution.

Teaching is for the most part a female dominated profession. As such, they have been less dependent as the bread winner for their families and have been more easily controlled by management (administrators). They have been less influential in making management type decisions and influencing management type actions such as might have prevented the development of the dogmatic mentality in our society. Additionally, there has been concerted influence against the teaching of moral and religious principles in public schools. Thus, the demise of our society cannot be blamed totally on the teachers, even though they have always been in the best position to have exerted the most influence on the trend. However they must take the bulk of the blame for not taking more dramatic action on the effects of the drift. The societal drift has been so gradual that I am not so sure that even today our society has recognized the demising characteristic of our dogma and its effects. I do feel that teachers should have recognized the reduction in learning characteristics of their students, especially considering the frequency and amount of testing of students that was conducted. Then, I don't want to get back into the finger pointing games. And, I realize that my comments are, to a large extent, "Teacher Bashing", this is not my intent. Even though it is important to establish a cause, I will leave it to the social scientist to resolve such issues. It is also realizes that, even teachers can suffer from deprived self-actualization.

Does a student have to love the teacher, the subject matter, or how the subject is taught in order to be successful in school? I don't think so. I have wanted to be a chemist for as long as I can remember. As I progressed towards a degree in chemistry, I came across teachers that were good, bad, devoted, prejudice and a few I wanted to believe were dumber than me. The one common thread that caused me to survive and eventually become a good chemist was that all my teachers, somehow, made me believe that to be successful I had to master the chemistry that was laid before me. I therefore felt good about learning it. It made me feel good because I had done well and was on my way to accomplishing my mission. In one sense, I was becoming self-actualized.

Why is it so difficult for our society to realize that we must first teach students to respect and believe in the art of self-motivation, the art of academic survival and above all that which makes them feel good about learning? When we accomplish this, the apparent effectiveness of the teacher becomes less important, and so does the need for many of the consultants and the many studies that are draining our teacher resources. The interaction of good teachers and students with a burning quest for the knowledge is unstoppable. We would no longer need to fire teachers who love teaching. We could use the resources to retrain any deficient teachers and make them better.

I have admitted to myself that what I have called analytical thinking is becoming somewhat condescending. Must teachers improve their motivation techniques? Absolutely! How many studies have we conducted, and how much money have we spent that have proved that the effectiveness of the teacher is one of the most important factors for school improvement? Not enough, but too many of the studied have been ineffective. The problem is that, most of the research has been directed towards motivating students, with placating techniques, rather than the academics and methods of teaching the subject matter. Student involvement is the battle cry of administrators charged with evaluating teachers. Student motivation and student involvement is also the fight song at teacher prep schools. And for students, the battle song is "It's boring".

About 85percent of students are actually too lazy to learn or do not have the motivation to really buckle down and study, not to mention how to teach a significant portion of the subject matter to themselves. Lazy students sounds like a strong and harsh condemnation, but we must remember that the laziness is something that we bred into our children.

I am comically reminded of a high school science teacher who had fabricated a water container he used to squirt water at students who were asleep or not paying proper attention in class. We did not have plastic water bottles or squirt bottles as some students would call them. He had made his own and it looked like a cow's tit. He could hit you from 25 feet away with that thing. One girl complained that he had messed her hair with his squirts of water. He smiled and hit her twice again.

The water squinting teacher is worth a few comments. In addition to me, he produced three graduate chemists from the same class in addition to countless others from other classes. And, I do not know that any of us really loved the dude. None disliked him and all respected him. He was brash and never hesitated to embarrass a student for non-performance. The embarrassing moments were never personal in nature, yet the students would know beyond a doubt, that they had done something wrong or did not meet his expectations, know exactly what was wrong, and when possible, how to correct it. All of us knew that we could not get by with wrong that he knew about. Was he a role model for his students? Not in the classical sense of today's role model as a professional athlete might be. Yet, he was an excellent teacher. His students and parents respected him and everyone knew not to cross him. He had gained respect and neither parents nor administrators would question his fairness about grades, or discipline related issues.

Recently, there has been lots of emphasis put on the need for role models, especially with the increase of fatherless homes. In most cases the role model will meet periodically with the student and try to become a friend and example for the student to follow. Some are successful but most are not, mostly for the same reasons that teachers have difficulty connecting with students. The role model would be much more effective if trained to identify the psychological needs of the student. The student needs are more related to his need for denied self-actualization than anything else. He does not need someone to tell him how to conduct his life. He feels that he already knows this. If he feels that he needs new direction, he needs to feel good about any new direction and the possibility of success that his advisor might give him. I do not want to be critical of programs and organizations that supply role models in an attempt to help students. But I am saying that they would be much more effective if training were involved. Role models picked at random of because they are successful at something may or may not be successful with a randomly selected student. Tutoring programs are a definite asset to students who need it.

Recently, there has been talk of neighborhood schools, more ethnic teachers which echo the student body, teachers which can better relate to the students,

teachers who can make subject matter more interesting to the students and a host of factors which made me think of the old separate but equal doctrine. Great, ideas but we all know that does not work. Besides not being equal, problems arise when students leave the neighborhood, and the dogmatic mentality of "Not like me" and biased competition sets in.

Who could really believe that charter schools could be different or produce better results than conventional public schools? Level the playing field and all schools would logically be the same. The proponents of charter schools should be ashamed of themselves. It is so obvious that there must be misguided motives associated with their advocacy. There is some logic that the super talented or the super motivated would be better off when grouped. But do we need a separate school to do this? Can we, with our dogmatic attitudes group fairly or do we really know how to be effective with our group selections?

We should take a look at public funds used for private schools and insure that charter schools are not unfairly funded. That is so unfair. But there is another side to this augment. How can we have the educational success exhibited by the private schools transferred to the public schools? What makes the differences in the schools? I think we all know the differences but are afraid to tackle the problem. Is it reasonable to think that we would ever level this playing field? Let the rich have their private schools. They have my congratulations because they have earned that distinction. But let's not try to gain the same advantage at the expense of our urban schools, and then proceed with misguided selection based on race, economics or neighborhoods etc. We can improve our urban schools and duplicate if not exceed the success of the private schools. But first we must rid our schools of the expensive consultants, and the neurotic comparison we make of each other, and teach ourselves and our children to do the morally correct things. Then we can educate our children in the best manner.

I am still analyzing a statement made to me by my fourth grade granddaughter. She said, "Grand Daddy I am good at math but I do not like it". Her comment connoted that she had the motivation to master the subject even though she did not like it. I loved her even more for saying it. Maybe genetics does have a place in school improvement (smile-smile). I am also reminded again of the student who after a start at learning checkers improved his game to almost perfection. What about my student, who was so elated with his learning, that he taught the concepts to the whole basketball team. Is it possible to direct some of our research dollars in this direction? I can say with certainty that the concept of grouping, as pedagogy advocates, is amethod for students to teach other students—a method I loved and did sort of embrace, is good. The problem, I thought, was the bad student (s) dominated and the groups became islands of disruptions. I really felt the student teachers, being unskilled at recognizing the ego effect, were victims of un-met self-actualization of the unlearned students they were trying to teach. Hold this mouth full for the teaching of self-actualization.

No one can argue against student motivation, effective pedagogue, or getting to know your students as methods to improve learning. Likewise no one can argue against teacher evaluations and the elimination of ineffective

teachers or better curriculum. The point is that we have been preaching, studying and spending money on improving these as remedies for years. And, by any reasonable measurement, our schools have gone backwards. As a nation our relative position in the academic world has dropped and our position as leader in the industrial world is in serious jeopardy.

If we are to execute a solution through education we must be very astute, creative and practical with our approaches.

CHAPTER V

Perception of Teachers

For the most part teachers are the unsung heroes of most school systems. Yet they are considered by popular belief, to be the purveyors of most of the problems with schools. Administrators and teacher educators express the need for more and better teacher training, elimination of teacher unions, reduced class size, better pedagogy, the need for a more uniform curriculum, problems with special education, better classroom management, better school atmosphere—and the list goes on to, occasionally, includes a need for better school management. But when teachers and their problems are looked at with a critical scientific eye a different view of their problems and needs emerge and several new theories emerge.

One thing for sure, the student song of boring teachers is one that should be erased and never uttered again. Almost any teacher trying to teach will be boring to some students and heroes to others. Boring is a dramatic excuse, created by students, to compensate for the pain of learning and their determination to not learn. It has led teachers to deviate from their natural methods of teaching and spend time, money and an enormous amount of energy at entertaining students. Some students will like the teacher for whatever the reason. Thus, in the eyes of some, there are good and bad teachers. This contention, i thought, was the beginning of the big debate on teacher proficiency but does not excuse teachers from any and all criticism.

Once the frustrations of trying to teach sets in, most present day teachers, especially of intercity students, appear to be resolved that the teaching of the defiant students was impossible. These theories suggest that teachers are the victims rather than the culprits. To their dismay, teachers have fallen prey to the apparent characteristics exhibited by the children and the inability of society to make the appropriate adjustments. Teacher unions, trade organization, and administrators have been of little or no help to the teachers because the prevailing theories and thus, most of their efforts at helping the teachers have been bases on invalid causes and the demons of teacher bashing.

The above contentions characterize our present day teachers who love teaching and love their jobs but are losing it. Their problems are interactive. The frustrations caused by neurotic, disgruntled students coupled with the loud voices of disgruntled parents and pushy administrators are daunting. Disgruntled parents often turn to administrators for help when problem arises. The administrators often do not analyze these problems but will approach the teacher, often with disdain leading to more frustrated teachers. Once the frustrations of trying to teach sets in, most present day teachers, especially of intercity students appear to be resolved that the teaching of the defiant students is impossible and most stop effective teaching.

These theories and the teachers themselves are easy targets of prey for critics as well as researchers. The lack of classroom management skills is the favorite target used by first echelon administrators who are usually responsible for discipline matters. The teachers, especially the more experienced ones become resolved that the best way to handle defiant student behavior is through appeasement. They have become very astute at alleviating rowdy and defiant student's problems using day to day remedies. Their remedies are time consuming at the expense of real academics and offer little or no effort towards improving student performance. The main goal of most intercity teachers is to get through the day.

On the other hand, students will observe the teacher, analyze and learn the habits of teachers with the skill of a seasoned research scientist and go into action with their own remedies, often at the expense of the teacher. There are far too many teachers who really like their jobs as teachers. But, because of the defiant rowdy and unmotivated students, they are finding their job frustrating if not impossible. Administrators tend to join with the pacifying teachers and do not require that they teach. They require only that the teachers keep order.

Students will observe the teacher, analyze and learn the habits of teachers with the skill of a seasoned research scientist and go into action with their own remedies, often at the expense of the teacher.

Teachers mollify the students with trivia work that the student can successfully do with little or no effort. This seems to pacify the students and they are happy with the apparent self-actualization that the easy work affords. Another approach is to simply entertain the students. Chemistry classes are always boring unless something burns. Math classes, because of their requirement for critical thinking, are just as bad for the students. Present day pedagogy dictates an interest approach at the start of each class. This technique appeared to serve the teachers well and some teachers would extent the interest approach, as cntertainment, for the whole period. The student voices expressing boredom and frustration with teaching are loud and clear.

Quiet students are often allowed to sit in the rear of the class and doodle as long as they do not disturb the class. Students learn quickly that this and a smile will please the teacher and they will pass the class.

I am still trying to analyze a documentary on education presented by MSNBC which depicted a fight between two girls in a 4th or 5th grade class. The girl on the winning side of the fight was about twice the size of the other girl and appeared to have started the fight. First, I question whether the parents of either child gave permission to air their children in such a vicious fight. Except for depicting the trials and tribulations of teaching, there was no other mention of the fight with in the documentary. Second there was a seam of students lined up as if they were waiting for something and the teacher was voicing displeasure of the students. In all the seams, the students appeared to be minorities. Most of the students in the depictions appeared to show strong nonverbal mannerisms of resentment. In these days of racial strife, i thought the television stations should reframe from depicting races in such negative light unless they are making specific reference to what they are depicting.

The problems of teachers are directly related to failing schools. Maybe we should call these "the practices of teachers" rather than "the problems of teacher". They raise the question, "What comes first, the chicken or the egg". Negative practices by teachers certainly do not improve the situations of poor student performance but it is not the true cause. The need for and the struggle for students to obtain self-actualization appears to be a main reason for defiant students, classroom management problems, low test scores, teacher frustration, high droop out rates(see appendix #), and a whole host of other problems related to the dilemma of poor performing schools. Educating teachers on the neurotic needs of students would, without a doubt help the situation but is not a total solution or guarantee to solve all the problems. Physiology and the neurotic needs of students is not a major item in the curriculum for teacher education, at least not in the form that it should be.

As I reviewed what I had written it all made sense to me. Our education system is one big interacting agglomeration of mess factors and it makes little sense to point fingers or try to determine how it all got started—by bad students, genetically inferior students, lack of student motivation, bad teachers, lousy administrators /poor managers, lousy parents, poorly funded education, poor teacher preparation and last but not least—politicians. All of these are factors in the mess and dooms day is just around the corner. In thinking about a solution, I cannot help but reflect on my own background—a poor black kid who somehow got out of the hood and manage to mingle with the rich and famous, the good, bad, ugly acting, the beautiful and the righteous. And, I have concluded that there is not a spoonful of difference in learning ability between any of us except for life's experiences and the interaction some people call luck and others may call divine interventions. Luck and Devine intervention, I will not touch because on the way from nothing to fame, a lot can happen that cannot be explained.

MOTIVATION

My analytical mind again kicked into high gear and I thought the best and most efficient way to interact with life's experiences or to optimize the life experiences for the best possible effect is through education. Here I thought "Dame Teachers". THEY COULD HAVE PREVENTED THE MESS WITH A LITTLE FORETHOUGHT.

Teachers have unfettered access to students for 12 of their formative years and for more effective hours per day than most working parents. If 10 percent of the teachers are bad teachers, 90% are good teachers and most are at least certified. Could we have more than 10 percent bad teacher? I don't think so. But, regardless, for the most part, I cannot think of any other entity that is in a better position to have affected or should have affected our way of life than teachers. And they have done what I considered an excellent job until lately—until the big interacting agglomeration of mess factors set in on our

85

society. History suggests that we formed a more perfect union, and became the most desirable nation on earth, through education, all after the exertion of our military might. Far too many people forget that our military might was built through education. Thus, the egg came before the chicken. My contention is that if teachers had exerted the proper influence on students, the present situation leading to our demise, should not have developed. Dam, I thought? What Happened? Now, I have begun to point fingers and it is looking in the direction of the teachers—for the cause and, hopefully, the solution.

Teaching is, for the most part, a female dominated profession. As such, they have been less dependent as the bread winner for their families and have been more easily controlled by management (administrators). They have been less influential in making management type decisions and influencing manage type actions such as might have prevented the development of the dogmatic mentality in our society. Additionally, there has been concerted influence against the teaching of moral and religious principles in public schools. Thus, the demise of our society cannot be blamed totally on the teachers, even though they have always been in the best position to have exerted the most influence on the trend. However they must take the bulk of the blame for not taking more dramatic action on the effects of the drift. The societal drift has been so gradual that I am not so sure that even today our society has recognized the demising characteristic of our dogma and its effects. I do feel that teachers should have recognized the reduction in learning characteristics of their students, especially considering the frequency and amount of testing of students that was conducted. Then, I don't want to get back into the finger pointing games. Even though it is important to establish a cause, I will leave it to the social scientist to resolve such issues related to cause and effect.

Does a student have to love the teacher, the subject matter, or how the subject is taught in order to be successful in school? I don't think so. I have wanted to be a chemist for as long as I can remember. As I progressed towards a degree in chemistry, I came across teachers that were good, bad, devoted, prejudice and a few I wanted to believe were dumber than me. The one common thread that caused me to survive and eventually become a good chemist was that all my teachers, somehow, made me believe that to be successful I had to master the chemistry that was laid before me. I could not blame the good, bad, or ugly teacher for my failure. I therefore felt good about learning their stuff. It made me feel good because I had done well and was on my way to accomplishing my mission. In one sense, I was becoming self-actualized as I progressed with success.

I want to mention another almost comical, yet sad, incident. It was the practice of administrators to conduct what they called "Walk-throughs" where a group of administrators would visit a class and observe what is going on. One day about five of them descended on my class. They would not explicitly tell teachers their purpose or the results of what they found. In this particular class there was a student I considered to be on the edge of being a derelict. Every day he would come to class and go to sleep, and sometimes he would sleep through several class periods. Why I tolerated him, I can never adequately explain because I knew it was a major violation of policy. I did feel sorry for him and he did remind me of a derelict that my mother would often feed and sometimes allowed him to sleep on the porch when the weather was bad. As a kid, I had lengthy conversations with him. He was a moral man and appeared to have a bit of formal education. As I recall, his major theme was "Do not go to jail".

One of the "Walk-through' administrators approached my derelict type student and asked in a loud voice as if she wanted the other members of her team to hear, "What's going on here?" He appeared to wake up and with glassy red eyes and in an equally loud voice, replied," I'm waiting for this (M.F.) to teach me his shit." Somehow, I was proud of him. I felt that he, at lease, expressed a purpose and was not totally oblivious to what was going on. I estimate that his real problem was drugs or maybe alcohol. As a teacher, you did not have the time or resources to really help him.

Why is it so difficult for our society to realize that we must first teach students to respect and believe in the art of self-motivation, the art of academic survival and above all that which makes them feel good about learning? When we accomplish this, the apparent effectiveness of the teacher becomes less important, and so does the need for many of the consultants and the many studies that are draining our teacher resources. The interaction of good teachers and students with a burning quest for the knowledge is unstoppable. We would no longer need to fire teachers who love teaching. We could use the resources to retrain any deficient teachers and make them better.

I have admitted to myself that what I have called analytical thinking is becoming somewhat condescending. Must teachers improve their motivational techniques? Absolutely! How many studies have we conducted, and how much money have we spent that have proved that the effectiveness of the teacher is one of the most important factors for school improvement? Not enough, but too many of the studied have been ineffective. The problem is that, most of the research has been directed towards motivating students, with placating techniques, rather than the academics and methods of teaching the subject matter. Student involvement is the battle cry of administrators charged with evaluating teachers. Student motivation and student involvement is also the fight song at teacher prep schools. And for students, the battle song is "It's boring".

About 85percent of students are actually too lazy to learn or do not have the motivation to really buckle down and study, not to mention how to teach a significant portion of the subject matter to themselves. Lazy students sounds like a strong and harsh condemnation, but we must remember that the laziness is something that we bred into our children, mostly by placing blame mostly on the teachers

I am comically reminded of a high school science teacher who had fabricated a water container he used to squirt water at students who were asleep or not paying proper attention in class. We did not have plastic water bottles or squirt bottles as some students would call them. He had made his own and it looked like a cow's tit. He could hit you from 25 feet away with that thing. One girl complained that he had messed her hair with his squirts of water. He smiled and hit her twice again.

The water squinting teacher is worth a few additional comments. In addition to me, he produced three graduate chemists from the same class and countless others from other classes. And, I do not know that any of us really loved the dude. None disliked him and all respected him. He was brash and never hesitated to embarrass a student for non-performance. The embarrassing moments were never personal in nature, yet the students would know beyond a doubt, that they had done something wrong or did not meet his expectations, know exactly what was wrong, and when possible, how to correct it. All of us knew that we could not get by with wrong that he knew about. Was he a role model for his students? Not in the classical sense of today's role model as would be professional athlete might be. Yet, he was an excellent teacher. His students and parents respected him and everyone knew not to cross him. He had gained respect and neither parents nor administrators would question his fairness about grades, or discipline related issues.

Recently, there has been lots of emphasis put on the need for role models, especially with the increase of fatherless homes. In most cases the role model will meet periodically with the student and try to become a friend and example for the student to follow. Some are successful but most are not, mostly for the same reasons that teachers have difficulty connecting with students. The role model would be much more effective if trained to identify the psychological needs of the student. The student needs are more related to his need for denied self-actualization than anything else. He does not need someone to tell him how to conduct his life. He feels that he already knows this. If he feels that he needs new direction, he needs to feel good about the new direction and the possibility of success. I do not want to be critical of programs and organizations that supply role models in an attempt to help students. But I am saying that they would be much more effective if training were involved. Role models picked at random of because they are successful at something may or may not be successful with a randomly selected student. Tutoring programs are a definite asset to students who need it.

Recently, there has been talk of neighborhood schools, more ethnic teachers which echo the student body, teachers which can better relate to the students, teachers who can make subject matter more interesting to the students and a host of factors which made me think of the old separate but equal doctrine. Great, idea but we all know that does not work. Besides not being equal, problems arise when students leave the neighborhood, and the dogmatic mentality of "Not like me" and biased competition sets in. I am not sure why our society continues with attempts to re-segregate our schools and sometimes I wonder that they were never really de-segregated.

Who could really believe that charter schools could be different or produce better results than conventional public schools? Level the playing field and all schools would logically be the same. The proponents of charter schools should be ashamed of themselves. It is so obvious that there must be misguided motives associated with their advocacy. There is some logic that the super talented or the super motivated would be better off when grouped. But do we need a separate school to do this? Can we, with our dogmatic attitudes group fairly or do we really know how to be effective with our group selections?

We should take a look at public funds used for private schools and insure that charter schools are not unfairly funded. That is so unfair. But there is another side to this augment. How can we have the educational success exhibited by the private schools transferred to the public schools? What makes the differences in the schools? I think we all know the differences but are afraid to tackle the problem. Is it reasonable to think that we would ever level this playing field? Let the rich have their private schools. They have my congratulations because they have earned that distinction. But let's not try to gain the same advantage at the expense of our urban schools, and then proceed with misguided selections based on race, economics or neighborhoods etc. We can improve our urban schools and duplicate if not exceed the success of the private schools. But first we must rid our schools of the expensive consultants, and the neurotic comparison we make of each other, the politics, and teach ourselves and our children to do the morally correct things. Then we can educate our children in the best manner.

I am still analyzing a statement made to me by my fourth grade granddaughter. She said, "Grand Daddy I am good at math but I do not like it". Her comment connoted that she had the motivation to master the subject even though she did not like it. I loved her even

more for saying it. Maybe genetics does have a place in school improvement (smile-smile). I am also reminded again of the student who after a start at learning checkers improved his game to almost perfection. What about my student, who was so elated with his learning and taught the concepts to the whole basketball team. Is it possible to direct some of our research dollars in this direction? I can say with certainty that the concept of grouping as pedagogy advocated as a method for students to teach other students—a method I loved and did sort of embrace, is good. The problem, I thought, was the bad student (s) dominated and the groups became islands of disruptions. I really felt the student teachers—leaders within the group, being unskilled at recognizing the ego effect, were victims of un-met self-actualization of the unlearned students they were trying to teach. Hold this mouth full for the teaching of self-actualization.

No one can argue against student motivation, effective pedagogue, or getting to know your students as methods to improve learning. Likewise no one can argue against teacher evaluations and the elimination of ineffective teachers or better curriculum or even placating type motivation techniques. The point is that we have been preaching, studying and spending money on improving these as remedies for years. And, by any reasonable measurement, our schools have gone backwards. As a nation our relative position in the academic world has dropped and our position as leader in the industrial world is in serious jeopardy.

If we are to execute a solution through education we must be very astute, creative and practical with our approaches.

CHAPTER VI

Better Identification of the Problem

Though not the total of the problems, our teachers have dropped the ball. Through complacency and the actions of strong unions, teachers bred incompetency within their ranks. They did not adequately identify what was happening to their students nor did they recognize the exponential decay in learning or the impact of what was happening within our society. They did not recognize the impact of strong parents wanting their children to go to Harvard via a bucket full of A+'s on their transcripts. The cry for greater parental involvement yielded more demand for A's and more by any means necessary. For too many parents saw parental involvement as a cry for better teachers and more A's for their children. And, too many teachers began to see minority students thru the eyes of public opinion. They saw minorities as lazy, poorly prepared, dangerous, and full of hopelessness and any number of traits rendering them un-teachable. But all that was needed was a teacher that was fair, caring, non-judgmental, demanding, tolerant and willing to believe they can teach them.

Teachers acquiesced to the ease of less than perfect teaching, and to administrators who felt that keeping the parents happy by handing out " A"s to those who

94

hollowed the loudest was a good thing. The problems caused by imperfect teaching, bred fertile ground for politicians. The politicians with their never ending need to curb the expanding cost of government and education began to shout loud and clear—Kill the unions, we need better teachers, and that integration and immigration was the cause of our problem.

The education marketers began to line their pockets thru new text books, new curriculums and all sorts of devices, shrewdly marketed as help for teachers and the new problems they were facing. The manufacturers of electronic teaching aids were having great success, sometimes with less than perfect, expensive and sometimes not necessary teaching aids. I hate to think of the money and the number of "Easy to Teach Devices" developed for the science teachers and science curriculums. Teachers gravitated to the devices, often without adequate training on the best methods of using them, breading more imperfect teaching.

New teachers were victims of the "How to teach" proper gander put out by for profit oriented research organizations. Maybe they did recognize that something was wrong and were searching for salvation. Most teachers, especially newer teachers and far too many administrators tended to migrate to "How to teach propaganda". Consider the follow excerpt from a "How to Teach" article designed to promote student motivation. The recommendations were;
Give frequent, early, positive feedback that supports students' beliefs that they can do well.
Ensure opportunities for students' success by assigning tasks that are neither too easy nor too difficult.

Help students find personal meaning and value in the material.

Create an atmosphere that is open and positive.

These suggestions appear as good general suggestions for most teachers but are not practical. With 183 students only the last item is practical. Creating a positive atmosphere is always a good idea. The other items are acquiescing to lazy students and the active engagement of these items on a daily bases requires too much teacher time and/or energy. I submit that students may know what has personal meaning, but only for their self and they do not know the real value of what they are asked to learn. Back in the day I would have walked out of every history and most English classes because, as a young student I did not like the subject matter, or the teacher. There is little doubt that had the teacher expended time and energy to convince me and her other 182 students, each with different interest, otherwise would have been a big waste waste. Additionally, these are the type items that make their way onto administrative check lists used with evaluating teachers.

Consider the following two additional excerpts from a "How to Teach "article asking students to analyze what makes their classes more or less motivating." Sass (1989) asks his classes to recall two recent class periods, one in which they were highly motivated and one in which their motivation was low. Each student makes a list of specific aspects of the two classes that influenced his or her level of motivation, and students then meet in small groups to reach consensus on characteristics that contribute to high and low motivation. In over twenty courses, Sass reports, the same eight characteristics emerge as major contributors to student motivation:

Instructor's enthusiasm
Relevance of the material
Organization of the course
Appropriate difficulty level of the material
Active involvement of students
Variety
Rapport between teacher and students
Use of appropriate, concrete, and understandable examples
Variety
I submit that the instructor's enthusiasm means the instructor's ability to entertain, relevance means whether the students like or dislike the material, appropriate difficulty level means hard or easy and so does student involvement and variety. The point is that teachers, in the midst of proper gander critical of their teaching, were constantly thrown off the track of what and how to teach.

Another point is that if the marketers of education aids have much to offer, why not put it into the teacher colleges where the teachers receive their initial training where proper use of the method can be taught to the teachers, leaving the practicing teachers to perfect their training in the class room. They should be free to practice and perfect their wares and should not need to be retrained. Likewise,

Administrators should consider other ways of updating their teachers rather than through the so called professional development. Professional development is far too expensive as it is practiced today. One method that would be much less costly might be through mandatory periodic recertification of teachers.

It is not my intent to minimize motivation. The point is that it has been over emphasized and teachers have been so engrossed with it that they have sacrificed teaching for the sake of motivating students.

The school of hard knocks teaches that students are motivated by a combination of success, confidence and ego, all born from within the individual. Without a witness, each of these factors is folly because the individual is not fully self-actualized in these matters until he is internally convinced of them. Good teachers realize this, either intuitively or have learned it the hard way. I am not sure what happened, but the old school teachers had gravitated to such methods as scaffolding, earned praise and do not forget <u>respect and the ability to inspire the student's confidence that the teacher can and will led them to success</u>. Most minority students enter the classroom with none of these and give the impression of not being motivated—a fact that most teachers do not realize.

As teachers dropped the ball, discipline problems began to surface, first in the inner cities, then in the elite suburban schools. Teachers and most of the public began to believe that their problems were caused by integration and immigration coupled with defective genetics. There was an increase of enrolment into newly created charter and private schools. The press begun to emphasize the problems and expand on the demons they thought were causing the problems, yielding press to all possible solutions that appeared controversial. The overall causes purported as true, were easy for the public to identify. They were excellent farter for the public and politicians looking for something to blame, to grab hold to for speech making purposes and were excellent conversation pieces for the general public.

Societal creep towards a more dogmatic public mentality was also an accelerating factor related to the problems. The agglomeration of interactions purported as causes, because of their number and complexity, were much more difficult to reconcile and caused tons of heated debate on needed corrective actions.

Research on methods for correcting our school problems increased and

Researchers began to line their pockets with money, mostly from grants and philanthropic organizations. Teachers became frustrated, mostly from the attacks on their profession which included many attempts to break their unions and even to fire teachers. And, as time passed, a

Consider the evolution of peer pressure. Following and emulating one's peers was once a natural first step in letting go of one's parents. But peer pressure today can be more like a mafia experience than part of a growth stage. It's powerfully organized around the Internet, utilizing such weapons as iPhones, iPods, and Facebook pages, and is further subsidized by the electronics, music, clothing, and cosmetics industries. A tremendous investment is involved in this peer-pressure network.

What used to be cliques and clubs has morphed into a huge "iCulture" whose influence indoctrinates self-centered and elite attitudes and values in young people that quite often undermine the purposes and authority of adults.

The shrinking influence of the American family and the loss of its support system—extended family,

neighborhood, church, community, and other endangered face-to-face institutions—leave no counter to this highly organized I Culture. Joe Gauld, Ed Week, Oct28,2010

Significant number of citizens began to believe the prober gander. A confusing interaction was the fact that some intercity students were highly successful while others were not. This interaction pushed public opinion strongly towards family values, family income, and other parental influences as causes for the problems. Thus, the cry for more parental involvement was born. Parental involvement involving their children was good for the overall problems. But it rapidly joined with the demons against teachers. Bad teachers became their battle cry and the reason their children were receiving dad grades, low test scores and were not being admitted to Harvard, Yale and MIT.

Another problem with educational research involves the amount of money spent on ethnic research and the results obtained. Studies have centered heavily on the habits, likes and dislikes, learning styles, religions, do's and don'ts, all related to methods that would allow teachers to get to know and better relate to the different groups. Second to these objectives is research directed at identification of the strengths and weakness and causes of variances between groups?

The most significant educational research findings, I feel, have pointed to economic disparity as the principle reason for performance differences between groups. Yet, we have concentrated on improving the group rather than eliminating the true cause of the disparity. My analytical mind again tells me that economic disparity is so ingrained in our increasingly dogmatic mentality that it will take years of proper political intervention to correct it. In some respects progress is, indeed, being made. The gap is increasing, and the disparity on the low end of the economic scale is increasing more rapidly than that on the high end. Consider the following.

If individual differences rather than group differences were looked at, I am sure we would see a broader distribution with the individual differences. Then we must ask ourselves, why we insist on evaluating groups according to some preconceived misconception. I am tired of looking at data evaluating, white, black, male, and female, various religions, or anything that we can identify as the other people effect. We should know by now that there are no white or black people and it appears as if the male and female species are evolving into one entity, especially with studies involving academics. We tend to evade reality by grouping before we do the analysis. Our tendencies to not group outside the preconceived norm are another testimony to our drift towards a dogmatic society.

This is practically true with studies involving economic disparity versus academic performance. In family such as mine where my father never earned more than $1.60 per hour and my mother never worked outside the home, yet six of six children obtained college degrees, would not correlate. A study of individual differences might show that some other variable would be more effective at identifying significance. Statisticians could have lots of fun playing with the multitude of variables that would be unleashed in a study of individual differences. More realistic collaboration between mathematicians and social scientist would be necessary. I also submit that the social scientist have dropped the ball with respect to regulating our society than have teachers.

In researching this book, I was amazed at how antiquated and misguided social research had become—lots of data but no real analysis.

Our students have begun to reap the benefits of frustrated teachers who are beginning to give up on teaching, and give grades to students for little or no real academic progress, or for placating gestures. Young college graduates are telling me that in order to get a job they must have a graduate degree and we are beginning to accept that as fact. We are teaching nothing in our high schools and because of a pyramid effect, not much in our undergraduate colleges. Thus, we must have a graduate degree to get a reasonable job. Our industrial companies are constantly complaining about the education of our graduates and are seeking students from abroad. Take a look at Appendix 3 which shows the percentages of students requiring remedial classes in math and English at the state's only junior college.

Consider the combination of frustrated teachers, antagonistic and finger pointing politicians, neurotic students with unrealized self-actualizations and all the psychotic traits this imparts, frustrated aggressive parents with dreams grandeur for their academically deficient children, all augmented by a social creep towards a more dogmatic society and societal economic turmoil and you have a Prelude to Disaster. More importantly, we must consider the generational effect on our society—the effect that multiple generations under the influence of this combination, has had on our society. This societal creep is just as problematic

CHAPTER VII

Teacher and Student Evaluations

The message to evaluate and fire teachers and tie their evaluations to student performances is loud and clear. It is even expressed by our federal government with their race to the top program. In attempts seeking consistence and fairness in evaluations, these programs have spun other movements such as those directed towards uniform curriculums and uniform evaluation methods. The race to the top program has led states to collaborate their efforts.

I feel it is a big mistake for states or agencies to band together their ideas for improving our schools. Such collaboration may make them feel better about what they are attempting to do. But from the get go, I have felt the idea behind the program was to stimulate creativity and ideas, hopefully based on research, that would lead to better teachers and better schools. Collaboration will reduce redundancy, but will also stifle the creation and diversity of innovative ideas. Consider what happens when students are restricted as to what they learn or the diversity of their thoughts or the diversity afforded by their diverse backgrounds. I submit that we may be riding on cement tires over rubber roads without the diversity afforded by the diverse thinking and learning involved by

all our students. I once asked my students to write about the reasons why rubber roads and cement tires would not be a good idea. I wish I could summarize adequately their individual ideas. Their ideas were amusingly diverse.

As a kid living in the hood, my brother and I would wash cloths once per week and our mother would insist that we rinse the cloth toughly or they would smell of the harsh caustic soap we used. Somehow I learned how to determine when the cloths were rinsed enough. This concept followed me into chemistry and led to significant developments related to micelle formation and the formation of roam in paints and grit formation in emulsion polymerization. In college, when the instructor explained the concept of micelle formation, I immediately understood and associated it with my experience washing cloths as a kid. The point of this story is that students learn from life experiences regardless of how trivial those experiences may appear. Some people will argue weather students from the hood would experience limited life experiences or just different life experiences. The real problem arises when the student experiences the same thing over and over again and is not afforded the true diversity that life should afford. In this respect, a uniform curriculum might be counter-productive. While such might not restrict what each student will learn, it would restrict the diversity of what society would learn. Wake up all you academic researchers. It is time to think a new way.

Absurd ideas such as firing of teachers, eliminating seniority, destroying teacher unions, and other aspects may catch on because of the perceived economic advantages of such actions. **But this action may also result in the hiring of different teachers trained by the same tired teacher colleges and more of the same results.** Diversity in teaching is as important as diversity in learning.

I believe that only teachers can teach and evaluate students. The old traditional test prepared by the teacher who teaches the class is a valuable tool to be used at the teacher's discretion with the evaluation of students. To put student evaluations in the hands of anyone but the teacher is a big mistake. The job of the administration should be to insure that the teachers teach to the best of their ability and to make it as easy as possible for them to do so. When the job of teaching becomes easy, more of their time and creative energy is freed and the teacher will be more creative and will become a more effective teacher, especially those that love teaching and learning. When we do not trust the teacher to teach and produce optimum results as only they can see, we are indeed on the verge of disaster. However when teachers are not producing optimum students, we are also on the verge of disaster, as may be the situation we are presently experiencing and must be corrected. "By Learning, You Will Teach, By Teaching You Will Learn" Latin proverb

Such collaboration as was developed with "Race to the Top" may make most feel better about increasing their chances for better schools or to win the money. But I feel the idea behind the program was to stimulate creativity through diverse thinking and ideas, hopefully based on research that would lead to better schools. Collaboration will reduce redundancy, but will also stifle the creation and diversity of innovative ideas. Absurd ideas such as firing of teachers may catch on because of the economic advantage of eliminating seniority and destroying teacher unions and catch on because of the political expediency afforded by our tendencies towards dogma, but may also result in the hiring of different teachers trained by the same teacher colleges and stagnant ideas.

Collaboration is good and it is difficult to argue against it. But, with issues such as uniform curriculum and standardized teaching methods, we should draw the line. I feel. With my experience as a research chemist, often involved with collaborations between different disciplines such as between chemist and chemical engineers, bio-chemist and physical chemist; the benefits of diversity were exceptional. Having said that; I will argue that uniform curriculums, developed beyond the basics, will seriously limit the diversity of learning, stifle creativity and the development of diverse learning.

It can be argued also, that the firing of so called bad teachers is a dad idea from a slightly different point of view. Remember that teachers are trained and certified by a diversity of states, universities and colleges. You would expect that their teaching styles would be different but not necessarily differently wrong. Would students benefit, differently but as good, from a chemistry teacher trained in bio-chemistry as opposed to physical chemistry or one trained in theoretical verses industrial chemistry who would more likely take more of a hand on approach?

With teaching, experience is golden. Thus, the role of teacher retention becomes extremely important. Our massive recruitment task becomes a key question. A new book by Katy Farber, <u>Why Great Teachers Quit: And How We Might Stop the Exodus</u> (Corwin) speaks powerfully to causes and cures for teacher attrition. It's a book that is very much of the moment in contributing to the national education policy conversation. Farber wonders: What if we shrink the recruitment problem by stopping the hemorrhage? In a recent speech in Arkansas, Education Secretary Arne Duncan said much the same thing. The Asia Society recently held an international symposium on teacher quality and they found that high-performing countries put much more energy into recruiting, preparing, and supporting good teachers—rather than on the back end by reducing attrition or firing weak teachers.

The one hang up that plagues the relations between the administration, the teachers and their unions is teacher evaluations. And, any good administrator must know that this contention breeds animosity, mostly because of mistrust and the lack of definition of a good teacher. This confusion has been fueled by public animosity against teachers. The more we try to define a good teacher, the more animosity we develop and the more administrators will like young teachers that can be molded and shaped by their personal image of a good teacher. This brings us to the point that the best teacher being the one that loves teaching, is properly trained, and teaches to the best of their ability.

The best administrator in this respect is one that can constantly hold the teacher's feet to the fire without being antagonistic. However, they must insist that the teachers do their jobs. By the way, a teacher's job is not to just teach the subject but to also teach the student low to learn the subject. I would like to relate an effective technique I have experienced at a central NJ high school about a hundred years ago.

1. All teachers were required to submit the next week's lesson plan and any test to the central office. The plans and test were filed by, department, subject and teacher.
2. Teachers were evaluated randomly by the principle, assistant principal, and department head with a target of at least one evaluation per month. The evaluation could consist of a review of the lesson plans and any test results, or an observation as determined by the administrator. Some teachers were observed more often, at the evaluators discretion, with care not to establish a pattern related to perceived teacher efficiency.
3. Each observation was followed with an open and frank discussion which included issues about lessons and lesson plan sequence and other issues related to efficiency, adherence to an established curriculum, test and test results, previous comments, changes and anything the teacher wanted to discuss. The administrator would review the teacher's folder prior to the meeting and have a good idea about what should have been taught. It should be noted that most teachers welcomed the reviews.
4. Only negative reviews (unsatisfactory notices) were given to the teacher in well documented format once per year

Such a procedure should satisfy most questions about teacher evaluations and as long as the curriculum was in place. It is felt that most teacher unions would buy in to this and be satisfied with any federal mandates along these lines. Teacher acceptance of this evaluation procedure is a testimony to good administrators.

If it is absolutely necessary for a national test to measure a school's overall effectiveness, a national test can be tired to any school when administered with a standard procedure. But is it absolutely necessary to test every year? Student and school testing has become big business and I question if some of the testing is instigated by the marketers of test and the analysis of test data might add that with the present state of debated about school improvement, too many test of students are given. Be reminded that tests only teach students how much they do not know. When test results are low and made public, it becomes a negative factor to student's motivation to learn. As a student, it is disheartening to read every day in the papers that you attend a low performing school.

The fact that our education system is in free fall is real. So is the fact that teachers are at the pedicel of the problem, mostly because teaching and learning is their prime responsibility. I feel it is their responsibility to ask for and demand whatever is necessary to get the help they need for maximum effectiveness.

Teacher unions should have been more helpful with demanding teacher help, with defining their roll, public relations and effectiveness as teachers. The government should be responsible for the administration and functioning of our education system. But it is the teacher who has first echelon responsibility for the product, i.e., learned students. Thus, the logic of our industrial management concepts would suggest that teachers be singled out in any search for defects. But, I feel that logic also suggest that the defective products are the students and we look at the students for the effective improvements. Logic suggests that we should look at what students are being taught as it is related to their learning efficiency. Their learning efficiency has been shown to be related to deficiencies in self-actualization which has been related to widespread discipline problems currently affecting learning. Logic suggests that we start with the teaching of self-actualization followed by how they are being taught. What the student learns, I feel, is a complex interaction of what the student wants to learn, and his life experiences, all shrouded within a core curriculum of diverse basics and the degree of optimizations of his life experiences. What the student wants to learn is strongly interacted with his degree of self-actualization.

RECONCILIATION AND ELIMINATION OF THE CAUSES

Change directed at school improvement must withstand the test of debate before it can withstand the test of time. And, we tend to be overly critical of proposed solutions to our school dilemma. The school dilemma, as defined and enhanced by time, has become so complex and intertwined with complex interactions, that perhaps, there is no apparent direct solution. Because I do not believe that a solution is impossible, I would like to say only that there might not be a solution in the conventional sense.

When scientists are faced with problems shrouded with multiple high order interactions as in the case

110

of proposals for school improvement, it is best to group and attack piles as whole entities rather than the individual variables from within the pile. In this case, the pile might be represented by the students, and our target must be to improve the performance of all our students. This presents us with an excellent opportunity because, we as teachers have unfettered access to the students. The problem with the grouping concept is with adequately identifying the groups, as have been eluded to previously with individual versus group differences. In this case, when race is identified as a group and does not exist for purpose of the study.

Logic and experience tells us that students learn best when they want to learn. This phenomenon returns us to the complex question "What makes students want to learn?" And, our conventional answers to this question have not withstood the test of time, mostly because our students are too diverse and complex. In this case, students as a group have not passed the group test which suggests that it would be more practical to study individuals rather than students as a group.

From my book "Prelude to Chaos"; Logic is the human endeavor more void of human interactions as it is born from within. Logic becomes more valuable when it withstands the test of time. In "Prelude to Chaos" It is further touted that deprived self-actualization and its effect on ego is the biggest deterrent to student learning. We cannot induce instant self-actualization into students but we can teach them, from an early age, the recognition of deprived self-actualization and the logic of its existence, its characteristics and effects on our psyche, its relationship to our ego, and all other aspects of deprived self-actualization.

I recall a skit where a student, about 8 years old approached a teacher with a burning question. The teacher walked away as if to ignore the student. He then returned to the puzzled student and asked "How did that make you feel when I walked away from your question?" The student said "I wanted to beat you up" indicating that it angered him. A discussion on the effect of the deprived answer ensued. This is an example of how self-actualization can be taught at an early age. It is obvious that with older students, more complex lessons on self-actualization can be pursued.

As a young minority growing up in the South during a time of intense racial strife, it was so easy to become bitter, and seek the easy way by not bearing the pain of learning. With today's students, when the pain of learning is too much to bear, the easy way out may be to quit or dropout. As I reflect of the more important lessons learned and the age that I learned it, this is what the great analytical mind says to me about the lessons. I am responsible for myself. No one but me is responsible for what I do or do not do with my life. It is difficult to determine actually when this lesson should begin. But it should be early and progress in intensity with age. The student must realize this before it is too late. For example, if a student drops out of school before he realizes that he and only he must bear the consequences of dropping out, in most cases, it is too late and restitution is much more difficult.

We must rid ourselves of the neurotic comparisons we make of each other because these comparisons are the bases for our ego derived frustrations. **Without these frustrations, we free ourselves and our energy to be creative from within ourselves and we are then free to be good citizens and, above all, our collaborative energies are free. The goal of being self-actualized is to lose the neurotic obsession with our self and the neurotic effects on our inner self derived from our feelings we gain from the "Other People Effect"—the neurotic comparisons we make that lead us astray. With the energy gained, we become free to love and feel concern for other people and grow from within ourselves. Once we lose the neurotic obsession we have liberated the forces leading to self-actualization— the road to unhampered growth. We must therefore teach the true meaning of the neurotic obsession—the effects of ego, both good and bad effects. The pride and motivations derived from ego should never be underestimated or diminished. Our students must be taught to feel good about learning because learning is from within us and this good feeling can replace any ill feelings and animosities we may have towards the accomplishments of others.**

Unfortunately, we have developed a culture where comparisons based on the demise and demonization of others is the norm. In doing so, we are drifting towards chaos. We must reverse this trend. We have learned and are beginning to believe, more and more that this demise is a natural way of life. We have taught ourselves to band together in groups for strength to facilitate the demise and demonization. We must reverse this trend. As a society we must UN-learn the belief that we are better because we have made others weaker and teach our children learn to grow ourselves.

Thru education, we must teach our children that we can only be better when we gain the love and respect of others. By teaching this to our children, we will teach ourselves how to love and respect others and to grow.

The concept of civilization goes far beyond people living together in harmony. The comparisons are made and progress is relative to our interpretations of these comparisons. Our standards of comparisons are so ingrained within our society we have begun to feel that they are HUMAN NATURE. We, as a people, must rid ourselves, thru education of these interpretations.

The following is an op ad which appeared in a major newspaper, written by a surpassingly learned director of a major middle school. He first expressed concern about the firing of Central Falls High School teachers, then expounded on the distorted history and problems with education, all based on how we feel about our relations with each other.

"The firing of teachers at Central Falls High School is the unfortunate but not unforeseen clash between the sad history of urban education in our country and the testing-dominated measures for accountability and high student performance in all of our schools. We are learning that there is much difficult work ahead if we are to free children in our cities from the stifling poverty that has been passed from one generation to the next.
First, we should understand that the context of the Central Falls problem lies in the evolution of public

education. Since the 1900s the story of our public schools has been one of increasing access on one hand, and the struggle to maintain high quality on the other. At the turn of the previous century, public schools were primarily for white advantaged children who could take time away from work or the farm to go to school. With child-labor laws, schools accommodated millions of less well-off children who were suddenly unemployed as well as uneducated. With the influx of these children, the schools began teaching life skills and vocational education, as well as traditional subjects built around the three "R's" and the classics. As waves of immigrants came into the country, public schools were asked to assimilate them into our culture.

After 1954, when the Supreme Court decided that separate was inherently unequal, black children flowed into the mainstream public-education system and public schools led the rest of the country in grappling with issues surrounding civil rights. With the passage of special-education laws in the '60s and '70s, once again, public schools were where social justice first appeared for people with disabilities, confronting some of our most basic taboos with the simple belief that the opportunity for children to achieve their potential extended to everyone.

Still, it was not until the early 1980s that the concept of "all children" appeared on the agenda of public education—first as a catchy slogan, and later as a serious mission. Until that time, children throughout the country often tried out school, only to learn that they really didn't fit the system because of inadequate preparation, unacceptable behaviors, undiagnosed learning disabilities, or cultural or religious differences.

Many found school just too boring. All these sorts of kids still exist today and it is the unfortunate tendency of many of us, including some educators, to blame the kids, or the parents, for their disengagement from school.

The "all-kids" agenda gained traction because it was no longer possible for most young people to lead a reasonably productive, fulfilling or happy life without the absolute minimum of a good high-school education. There are very few skills or trades that, once learned, will sustain a person for life. Instead, students need to learn how to learn again and again.

Not surprisingly, the system we built over the past century is kinder and more generous to children of advantage than to those who grow up in poverty. Today, our public schools are not "the great equalizer" as Horace Mann suggested long ago. Instead they tend to reinforce the inequities handed out at birth. Once again, nothing about this should shock us.

Having limited opportunity is simply what it means to be poor.

In many of our urban schools, the students who dropped out yesterday are the parents of our children today. We cannot expect these children to exhibit behaviors never learned in the first place. Few students have large vocabularies enriched by educated parents in homes filled with books. Many lack the intellectual curiosity to question and explore the world beyond their TV screens or neighborhoods. They often lack the skills to persevere through the frustration brought on by academic problems. Their attitudes and habits of mind are developed for the challenges on the streets of their neighborhood and not necessarily those of the classroom.

But these are our kids, and one benefit of federal and state efforts to make better schools is that, at least on paper, we are talking about reform for all kids. It is unfortunate that we measure the quality of schools with the blunt instrument of standardized tests, which may be most unfair to many urban children who are culturally distanced from the test. At the same time, as educator Deborah Kenny suggests, students should not be satisfied with merely passing a standardized test.

However, what may be more harmful to our children is letting more time go by before we accept the challenge to do whatever it takes to help them succeed. No longer can we make excuses about the children not fitting the schools. We know who they are, as we have for decades. It is up to us, the adults, to make sure that the schools fit the children. We must take on the institutional inertia that has been dragging down schools, especially high schools, for too long. I do not know whether or not our country is ready to do whatever it takes, especially for youth who are generally deemed to be "other people's children."

We will see what happens as the struggle for all kids and high quality continues.

Certainly, one of the ironies of the whole situation is that the very institution regarded as being comfortable with mediocrity is demonstrating the kind of tough accountability that is lacking on Wall Street, in politics and in sports."

This op ad appears shrouded in logic. I love the writer of this op ad as he echoes some of concepts of this book such as the generation effect. But, I draw the line with his references to (1) schools reinforcing inequalities handed out at birth (2) his interpretation of the phrase "separate but unequal", (3) schools accommodating less educated and that it is up to us to insure that the school fit the children, 4. To have limited opportunity means to be poor, and 5. Students who dropped out yesterday are the parents of today's students. Maybe this is just another example of our schools showing us how not to confront a serious challenge and base our actions on feelings from within ourselves based on actions that affect us and as individuals and that we can act on as individuals.

As a product of the segregated south, I can assure all that there was nothing inferior about these products, except for the lack of equal opportunity.
Fortunately, this op ad does not represent the feelings of all teachers of urban students. But, I feel it represents the feelings of far too many people charged with equal impunity and education of all students within their influence. My analytical mind tells me the author has given up on teaching a significant portion of his students mostly because of miss conceptions about the characteristics of the inner city students and their problems.

It is difficult to convince our society that intellectual inferior people are few and far between. Our definition of intelligence has also somehow become distorted. In my earlier high school days there was a student that most students considered dumb. Retard was not in our vocabulary. He had a twitch. Students and teachers considered him the dumbest in the school until someone pointed him to the wood shop. He started making furniture and now owns a multimillion dollar furniture manufacturing company. He must have at least learned how to make and count money. He still twitches.

Our parents taught us to remember that whatever life deals us, we must do the best we can with it. Our treatment of so called special education students is somewhat misguided. We must teach them to deal with their condition as they also must learn that they are also responsible for themselves. I agree that they should be main-streamed—put into regular class rooms and if they present a discipline problem, they should be treated as every other student. Only severely handicapped students should be segregated. I feel their behavior is a learned for the most part. However there are definitely some characteristics that require special consideration, treatments and segregation. The point is that most students labeled as special education have been misdiagnosed.

I can recall another student who on most occasions refused to do her homework. One day, about mid-semester after being chastised about her homework and receiving an F, she asked, "Has anyone told you I am mildly retarded?" I told her yes, and proceed to lecture her on making the most of whatever life dealt her. She never missed another assignment and passed the course.

To convince our society of the need to change our so called human nature is a formable yet, achievable task. Simply by measuring our progress based on the demise of others, simple mathematics and logic tells us that in the game of winning and losing, half will win and half will lose and the chaotic fight will start over and over. If we take out the losers in the fights, our civilization will eventually be reduced to zero.

According to Horney, even with a pervasive uncertainty about others, a neurotic person may be able to give a fairly accurate description of their behavior and even of neurotic mechanism if he is trained in intelligent observation of others people. This suggests that neurotic tendencies are reversible through education. Thru the logic of education, we can and must do this for our children.

Another major problem is teacher burnout. Within high schools, there are numerous problems, most of which have been alluded to in previous units of this book. Of these problems, discipline is the most tenacious problem but the psychological effects brought on by the press, politician, and the public are collectively more disheartening to teachers. The discipline problem is solvable through leadership and the teaching of self-actualization.

At the elementary school level, the day to day grind, with children whose mentality presents no real mental challenge to the teacher, yet are part of the constant daily grind, presents other causes of teacher burnout. At the high school level, every time the bell rings, the teacher gets a new batch of kids and sometimes a new subject to teach. This breaks the dullness of teaching and helps prevent teacher burnout.

At the elementary level, the same teacher teaches the same kids every day, all day. And, the curriculum is pretty much set for elementary schools with English, math, art, music, etc. in the forefront. Why not have a specialist teach each subject and have the students change classes somewhat like the high school students.

I can recall another incident with my 4th grade grand who was demonstrating the difference between compression and tension. For compression, she showed the palms of both her hands pressing against each other. For tension she showed her two index fingers pulling against each other. I attempted to show her the relationship of tension and compression by explaining to her that the index fingers pulling at each other was actually compression also because they were pressing against each other. She would not accept my explanation and told me that her teacher had told her and explained to her how tension was different from compression. My son who is well-educated in a nontechnical field felt that her explanation was adequate for a third grader (smiles).
I feel that if she had been taught the concept by a more technical teacher, the somewhat distorted misconception could have been avoided. My grand's misconception will no doubt follow her into college if not beyond.

My recommendation is that students in the elementary grades be taught by teacher specialist as do high school students. Why can't they change classes between subjects just as high school students? They could then receive more specialized instructions in at least the core subjects. The only rational behind the present system is that the present elementary teachers are trained as specialist in early childhood development. Why can't they be trained as both—in academic specialties and in early childhood?

TEACHING OF SELF-ACTUALIZATION AND OTHER CONCEPTS

At the present rate of drift towards a dogmatic society, the present rate of decline towards our education chaos is inevitable. To reverse these trends is a formidable task. While numerous factors are contributing to these declines, and most are interactive and difficult to define, all are related, totally, to our mentality as a society. There are no magic pills to take or tangible changes to our environment that we must make. The teaching of self-actualization within our schools is proposed as a means of improving our mentality and way of life. It is the most practical and efficient method of making the necessary changes to educate and convince our society that without these changes, disaster is ineffable.

We must start at an early age to instill in our children the concepts that the inner strength and accomplishments derived from that inner strength is what greatness is all about.

The goal of being self-actualized is to become all that you want to be, think you can be, and feel you should be but never at the expense of another. To create self-actualized citizens, we must condition our society thru our students to lose the neurotic obsession with ourselves and the neurotic effects on our inner self derived from feelings we gain from the "other people effect"—the neurotic comparisons that are ego driven. To do this we must, therefore, teach the true meaning of the neurotic obsessions and their effect on our lives—their innermost feelings, first, to our students. The rate of matriculation into our society is debatable. But beyond a doubt, other entities' such as civic and religious groups, endowed with these concepts can accelerate the matriculations.

We are a nation of emigrants, initially founded on the belief that we have the unalienable right to life liberty and the pursuit of happiness. Over the years our population has grown and our founding concepts have been infiltrated, by tendencies towards a more dogmatic mentality, by increases in immigration whose concepts of society might be different from those of our founding fathers. Sometimes I cringe when I hear of talk of modifying our constitution. One only needs to think of the confliction concepts in the press when almost any issue in government is raised. Our thoughts are not always that of our founding fathers.

In the teaching of self-actualization, it is important to teach how to identify and know the effect of the neurotic comparisons we make of each other. Otherwise, the student will not believe the overall concept is valid. While enrolled at our local university, trying to become a real certified teacher, I was asked what, I think, the teacher thought was one of those critical thinking questions. I gave my answer which the teacher did not like as she assumed was incorrect. She let me have one of those embarrassing denials of my answer which I felt was absolutely correct. I retaliated but slightly rephrased my answer. With a look of obvious amazement, she replied "Dam, I guess I never expected such a sophisticated answer. You are absolutely correct". I was elated that she accepted my answer, but being a minority, I was embarrassed that she did not expect a sophisticated answer. I was, no doubt, the oldest and most experienced in the class.

I can also recall numerous incidences, as a young chemist at meetings when I had contributions to make and was completely ignored; mostly it was believed that I had nothing to contribute. Both the company and I were short changed. These concepts must be part of the curriculum.

Adults and perhaps high school students are the groups more accustomed to competitive environments. With these groups, the concept that self-actualization must be born from within is not easily sold, mostly because of the neurotic comparisons that they are accustomed to making—the competitive drive that most feel will yield greatness . Most of our present citizens feel that their gain must create pain for someone else. The opposite of this concept is not easily rationalized. Competitive shame hurts and its relief is more easily obtained at the at the expense of others. We have taught ourselves that this is the natural tendency. Some may call it human nature. But we must teach that true pride is derived only from true accomplishments from within and by oneself. In a foot race, you must run faster than your competitor. There is no other way to win. You should never win the race by tripping your competitor.

Another problem for our schools is the influx of people who are different, especially people from third world countries, and the influx of people from the hood (other minorities within this country) where competition and survival are ominous and where the mentality is naturally more dogmatic. Such influx only adds to our naturally occurrence of societal drift towards a more dogmatic mentality. Therefore, classes in self-actualization should be mandatory for all immigrants. Besides adding impetus to our already existing dogmatic society, immigrants add distortions to our political climate as was created by the founders of our constitution. Remember that the immigrants who founded this country also developed our system of ideals, our system of justice, morality, devotion, and for the most part our religions and mentality as Americans. The newer immigrants bring with them the mentality more aligned with the current mentality of their country, which, in most cases is different. Thus, classes in self-actualization as originally defined here, is in order.

As in **Prelude to Chaos** caution is advised on the relationship of self-actualization to morality as related to religion. We must not approach self-actualization in a moralistic manner or try to instill religious-moralistic principles onto our students. If religion and moralistic principals must be dealt with, and it does, it is far better to only interpret the morality rather than develop it. Morality, in the eyes of Christians as well as any number of other religions, is such an intense and emotional issue that it would take away and distort the true objectives of teaching self-actualization and its relation to the inner self. Maintaining the competitive nature that most people feel is innate to humans is extremely important in developing the concept. The concept of competing within one's self to improve on or accomplish objectives must replace dogmatic competition.

History tells us the competitive drive can lead to empty success when obtained at the expense of others or from unfair advantages. The athletes who uses prohibitive steroids or the successful business man who gains great wealth by unscrupulous means will end up with an empty shell regardless of how great that the initial ambiance may be. The politicians who gains great power, money and fame, are often not happy and will seek more and greater satisfactions thru unlawful greed, often infidelity, risky activity, or some endeavor that they feel will yield greater satisfaction, often thru greater recognition of their invincibility or super powers. Some writers have called these the "Demons of Success", but are actually the results of un-realized self-actualization and the neurotic tendencies that develop within them.

I cannot help but think of Tiger Wood. He had gained great wealth and success, was recognized as the greatest golfer of all times, had a wonderful and "Hot" wife, and was the envy of most men. Something must have been missing from his life. Does it matter whether his yearning for additional self-actualization was learned, innate or enticed? The demons gained control.

How about Bill Clinton? Self-actualized people, weather adults or students, are vulnerable for dogmatic manipulations by un-actualized people and sometimes will appear as the perfect target for unscrupulous opportunist. Moral character should be emphasized when teaching self-actualization; mostly because enticements are often swathed within creature comforts. Since self-actualization is bred from within, students must remind themselves that they are the real victims of deprived self-actualization regardless of the origin. Enticement is no excuse for a wrong act. The announcement by "Flip Wilson "The devil made him do it" is no excuse.

126

We must develop within our children as early as possible, a sense of how to recognize, and be aware of the demonic demons, their causes and above all, and the consequences of competitive strife. Be reminded that competitive strife is good, as long as it is from within, with the objective of improving our self and items we have internal control over and that do not take away from or add to another's competitive downfall or implant grief to others.

Note the following quote from Horncy. "Under inner stress, a person may become alienated from his real self. He will then shift the major part of his energies to the task of molding himself, by a rigid system of inner dictates, into a being of absolute perfection (as he sees himself). For nothing short of god like perfection can fulfill the idealized image of himself and satisfy his pride in the exalted attributes which he feels he has, could have or should have" (Horney, 1942).

Embedded in this quote is the feeling of entitlement to additional fulfillment.

This quote exalts the demons of success and perhaps our drive towards success. Unfortunately, it has also driven us towards our dogmatic society. This can and must be avoided. We must teach that the struggle for success is good, but must be ingrained with compassion for our fellow man; our environment and all that will negativity affect our fellow men.

Also embedded with compassion for our fellow man are several concepts related to morality, most religions and our system of justice. No one can deny that, when self-actualization is truly developed within one's self, it is truly related to the morality and religious concepts. Nor can anyone deny the multitude of interactions involved in the study of these concepts, especially when drifts towards our dogmatic society are factored in. It is, thus, in the context of self-actualization—the relation of man to his inner-self which we must teach our children. *It will help tame our thoughts, actions and our drive towards that dogmatic society which is destroying us.*

The concept of self-actualization goes much beyond competitive drive. It is ingrained in our psychic, and is gaining more and more impetus into and is distorting our political philosophy. For example it is becoming more difficult to argue the concept of government entitlements without enraging the resentment of "Lazy looking for something for nothing citizens". Most can only see the hardship that that the lazy people imposes on the good hard working citizens and blinds us to the true benefits and original benefits of entitles. Likewise, because of deprived self-actualization, some citizens may seek the benefits of the entitlements, feeling that their deprived self-actualization was caused by someone other than themselves. Here, we have two additional reasons to teach self-actualization.

The age appropriate pedagogy and curriculum for the teaching of self-actualization should be developed by the teacher prep schools in collaboration with other departments within their college, such as the psychology department. I have listed the principles, I feel, have the most profound effect on students motivation and desire to learn. They are also based on the concept that students like to learn, want to learn and we as a society have created these as barriers to learning. It is thus, up to our teachers to remove these barriers to children's learning, take charge of the child's learning and to teach them the concepts involved. And, the most important lesson that must be taught is how to teach themselves. By teaching this lesson, we create lifelong learners. Most of the following list will have application to the teaching of any subject.

<u>Trust in the teacher</u> Remember that most students will enter the class with distrust if not fear, of the teacher. To actively search for this characteristic is too much of a burden on the teacher and detracts from teaching. But, the teacher must be trained in how to readily recognize these manifestations and take the appropriate actions.

<u>Failure without hope of restoration</u> Learning is painful for most students, as it should be, and failure is even more painful and will happen. Teachers must instill the necessary fight and drive to be successful into the students. When the press, teachers or any other faction advertise the negative aspects of a school, a class or an individual they are advertising failure which will grow a deterrent to learning through a feeling of hopelessness. Rather than have the student feel that a lack of drive is some type genetic defect and is the reason for failure, encourage the student to get up and fight. In order to get up and fight, the student must feel there are hope and a reason to try again. Students will want to blame everybody but themselves for the failure and teachers must attack this tendency. Generally, students like to be challenged. But they also like to be successful. Judging the sensitivity of the student is extremely important. But do not be afraid to challenge because failure is easy to repair when it is not accompanied by humiliation.

<u>Invisibility</u> When fear strikes, and it does quite often, students will want to become invisible. Attack this tendency with passion and sensitivity or it will increase.

With most invisible students, it is a good idea to approach them with topics they are likely to be successful with. Give them a chanced for positive self-actualization.

Not to worry because someone will do it for me the so called good teacher will easily become prey to this concept. Contrary to popular belief that the chalk and talk concept is bad pedagogy, students love a good lecture and will beg, "Just teach us". Sometimes, this is good. But the best and most effective teaching method is the discovery method—the student teaches himself. This method provides the most pride in learning and self-actualization for the student. The critical criteria for the teacher is when and how to give in with help or to provide the easy way out. The answer is never. Instead, the teacher should guide the student to the answer. Thus, the discovery method is still realized.

Group teaching when students work in groups and teach each other, learning is more efficient. However, it can easily turn to a disaster. The dynamics of the disaster have more to do with the group dynamics, sort of the same way that the dynamics of student to teacher are related. When the group dynamics become a source of denied self-actualization, or deflated ego, problems will ensue. Be reminded that un-actualized students are prone to deflated ego, especially when there is a super star within the group. Thus, it is a good idea to keep the groups, somewhat, composed of equal talents or to periodically remix the groups.

Challenging Students Never challenge an individual student. Challenge the whole class. It is well documented that students like challenges and respond well to them. However their response to them is immediate, short lived and often emotional. By challenging the whole class, the student is free to choose his moment of glory without the emotions of failure which are counterproductive to learning. Student's feet should be always held to the fire and pressured to learn and produce results.

<u>Keep expectations high</u> The student must Know that you have high expectations of them. And, the expectations are most effective when directed at the individual rather than the whole class. Individual expectations provide greater self-actualization opportunities. High expectations of the whole class must also be maintained but, is not as effective.

<u>Controversial topics</u> Do not avoid controversial topics. Approach them with openness and with pros and cons, letting the students express themselves with their own pros and cons. Students love controversial subjects. But caution is advised. Such topics must be controlled. Otherwise your class will turn into one big debate where students will strive to outshout each other and where nothing will be learned.

<u>The Mindset of Teaching</u> Scientist will do things the same way and get the same results. Teachers can do the same thing from Day 1 to Day 2 and the results are different. Working with students requires being on your toes, staying flexible and thinking ahead. When teaching, you are always engaged, in and out of school. There is very little time that you are not plugged in. Teaching is a job you take home both mentally and physically. Every action you give students is a reaction from you—you must teach, plan, grade, review and re-teach all day, every day. Patience, understanding and control of your emotions will play an important role in keeping your influence positive—even when you're not feeling that way. It is extremely important that you resist the dogma of expediency, especially when

it is counterproductive to good teaching.

Stay Upbeat When teaching self—actualization and other subjects which may be controversial, students tend to be distracted by topics they inwardly disagree with. The teacher should provide for revisiting such topics after appealing to a different logic of the subject.

It is unfortunate that discipline problems in our schools have progressed to the intolerable level. Ego and denied self-actualization have been identified as the underlying factors related to this problem. Since self-actualization is an innate factor, when denied, it is important that a means of reestablishing the self-actualization is provided. Several comments relating to this phenomenon is important to emphasize.

Remember the twitching student who became a famous furniture manufacturer. It is not unusual that student who is denied self-actualization will go into something resembling isolation. Often this will free their mind and they will have an excess of free time. Often, if they are not too frustrated, they will seek out something they like such as playing a musical instrument, an individual type sport, reading or writing poetry. Usually, they will perfect this endeavor and become extremely good at it. Remember the checker playing student who I taught to play checkers who became better than me.

In the high school that i attended, our band was the best, winning multiple state championships. As I can recall, the band director could not keep the students out of his practice room and the students would fight for the few available instruments to practice with. Music was one of the few means of self-actualization available to students. In far too many of our schools today, music and many other extracurricular activities have been discontinued for economic reasons. This is a big mistake. Its effect on school discipline is not so subtle and has not been realizes by school administrators.

The effect of denied self-actualization has not been realizes by school administrators and by many social scientist is not so surprising since there are so many avenues for denial and for reestablishing it. But we should be reminded that denials are more frequent, consistent and intense in urban areas. And, this tendency is increasing and spreading in suburban areas.

Recently, I was watching reruns of Sole Train on television, originally recorded from the early 70's to late 80's. Besides noting the differences in dance, music and dress styles, I noted a distinct difference in demeanor (facial expressions) of the dancers. Some of the earlier years, the dancers were more confident as expressed by their facial expressions and bold dance movements. In some of the latter years, their facial expressions became more pensive, even though all appeared to be enjoying themselves. One might ask how so much can be ascertained from facial expressions. Remember the earlier comments on eye contact? And remember the comments about how students will study a teacher with the skill of a research chemist and the fact that Perry Mason (Reruns are still on television) and even real lawyers, would observe the demeanor of juries as they descended from the jury room and try to predict their verdict? People are still doing this. We would call it "Reading" someone. Thru denied self-actualization, we have given this skill to certain students. Students who are denied self-actualization are more dependent on skills considered by most to be unscientific to make decisions. But the truth is that they have horned and fine-tuned their sense of observation out of necessity.

The latter years were characterized by the introduction of "Rap Music" and the decrease in formal music classes in our high schools. Rap was much easier to accomplish and more students were adapting this as a form of musical expressions and, hence, self-actualization. I might also add that it INTRODUCED THE DEMISE OF many things I LOVED—TRADITIONAL EXPRESSIVE MUSIC, open and honest expressions, the earnest debate, the comradely of true friendship; all based of love from within. Could all this be the results of an increase in denied self-actualization?

One last comment about discipline problems. When outward discipline problems and discipline of the mind are considered separately, two distinct and separate problems are presented. While both are caused and enhanced by denied self-actualization, discipline of the mind is more learned and the result of conditioning to the pain of learning. The learning of difficult subject matter exerts pain on the psyche and is something that young people will naturally avoid. To enhance the motivation to learn difficult subjects, the teacher must cultivate a love for the subject matter, an overt reason to learn the subject matter or establish a dramatic consequence of not learning the subject matter. Denied self-actualization could be a motivating factor in the learning of difficult subject matter. However it must be realized that encapsulated with such motivation is personal rational to not learn. For example, if you are part of a math class where most of the students are learning, you would be motivated to learn. If you are part of a class where it is accepted that math is difficult and most of the students are accepting of the fact that math is difficult, self-actualization would not be a motivating factor.

EPILOGUE

May all the Gods bless you with understanding of these words as they are the essences of our being—the culmination of what we were intended to be.

Once the greatest nation on earth, we have, by some unknown demonic force, made a wrong turn, and we are headed towards disaster. Our misdirection is leading us toward a dogmatic mentality resembling neurosis, which within itself, is reversible. Our misdirected mentality is not as obvious to the bulk of our society as it is shrouded in what we consider as natural tendencies of selfishness, egotism, misguided ambition and complacency. There is ample evidence that demonic neurosis is rapidly spreading within our communities and because of the impact on our progress as a people, is pegged "A Prelude to Disaster". Our dogmatic drift to disaster is accelerating at an exponential rate, mostly because our neurotic tendencies are shrouded in a form of paranoia and blame. As such, our society is deteriorating.

The most logical direction changer for our delusion is our education system which is also presently in a state of turmoil. Realizing that today's children are tomorrow's leaders, we have, with these words, first tied to capture the extent of our dilemma thru graphic portrayal of our present existence within a typical urban inner-city school. Priory knowledge, life experiences, logic and intuition have shown the correlation of our dilemmas and their solutions thru education of our children—our future leaders.

Our efforts at redirecting the mentality of our youth have been hampered by a generational effect of dogmatic mentality. Our neurosis has further affected our educational and political governess to the extent that our education system deteriorating further. Our position as a world leader has been compromised.

Thru education, we must reverse these trends and rebuild our position as a world leader. We must first recognize, un-learn the belief that we are better because we have made others weaker and learn to grow from within ourselves. We, as a people, must rid ourselves of this neurotic obsession and become self-actualized.

Within these words, sound recommendations for accomplishing this task have been made. However the formidable task of convincing our educational governess may not have been realized, as it is, within itself, shrouded in the generational politics of ego, selfishness and economics. But, by teaching our children the benefits and principles of self-actualization and how to recognize the effects of denied self-actualization, progress towards the desired end will be made.

Wake up all you teachers. It's time to teach a new way and build a new nation.

APPENDIX I

Theory of Neurotic Needs from Internet

While debatable, many agree that Horney's theory of neurosis is the best that exists today. She looked at neurosis in a different light, saying that it was much more continuous with what we call normal life than other theorists believed. Furthermore, she saw neurosis as an attempt to make life bearable, as an interpersonal controlling and coping technique.

Horney thought it a mistake to think that a neurosis in adults is caused by abuse or neglect in one's childhood. She, instead, named parental indifference the true culprit behind neurosis. The key to understanding this phenomenon is the child's perception, rather than the parent's intentions, she said. A child may feel a lack of warmth and affection if a parent, who is otherwise occupied or neurotic themselves, makes fun of their child's thinking or neglects to fulfill promises, for example.

Using her clinical experience, Horney named ten particular patterns of neurotic needs. They are based on things that all humans need, but that are distorted in some because of difficulties within their lives. As she investigated them further, she found that she could clump the ten into three broad coping strategies.

The first strategy is compliance, also known as the moving-toward strategy or the self-effacing solution. Most children facing parental indifference use this strategy. They often have a fear of helplessness and abandonment, or what Horney referred to as basic anxiety. This strategy includes the first three needs: the need for affection and approval, which is the indiscriminate need to both please others and be liked by them; the neurotic need for a partner, for someone else to take over one's life, encompassing the idea that love will solve all of one's problems; and the neurotic need to restrict one's life into narrow boarders, including being undemanding, satisfied with little, inconspicuous.

Horney's second broad coping strategy is aggression, also called the moving-against and the expansive solution. Here, children's first reaction to parental indifference is anger, or basic hostility. Needs four through eight (of Horney' 10 patterns of neurotic needs) fall under this category. The fourth need is for power, for control over others, and for a facade of omnipotence. Fifth is the neurotic need to exploit others and to get the better of them. Another need is for social recognition and prestige, with the need for personal admiration falling along the same lines. The eighth neurotic need is for personal achievement.

The final coping strategy is withdrawal, often labeled the moving-away-from or resigning solution. When neither aggression nor compliance eliminates the parental indifference, Horney recognized that children attempt to solve the problem by becoming self-sufficient. This includes the neurotic needs for self-sufficiency and independence and those for perfection and unassailability.

While it is human for everyone to have these needs to some extent, the neurotic's need is much more intense, Horney explained. He or she will experience great anxiety if the need is not met or if it appears that the need will not be met in the future. The neurotic, therefore, makes the need too central to their existence. Horney's ideas of neurotic needs mirrored those of Adler in many ways. Together, Adler and Horney make up an unofficial school of psychiatry and they are often referred to as neo-Freudians or Social Psychologists.

APPENDIX II

Self-actualization

Self-actualization is a term that has been used in various psychology theories, often in slightly different ways (e.g., Goldstein, Maslow, Rogers). The term was originally introduced by the organismic theorist Kurt Goldstein for the motive to realize one's full potential. In his view, it is the master motive—indeed, the only real motive a person has, all others being merely manifestations of it. However, the concept was brought to prominence in Abraham Maslow's hierarchy of needs theory as the final level of psychological development that can be achieved when all basic and mental needs are fulfilled and the "actualization" of the full personal potential takes place.

SELF-ACTUALIZATION IN GOLDSTEIN'S THEORY

According to Kurt Goldstein's book The Organism: A Holistic Approach to Biology Derived from Pathological Data in Man, self-actualization is "the tendency to actualize, as much as possible, [the organism's] individual capacities" in the world. The tendency to self-actualization is "the only drive by which the life of an organism is determined."[1] Goldstein defined self-actualization as a driving life force that will ultimately lead to maximizing one's abilities and determine the path of one's life; compare will to power.

SELF-ACTUALIZATION AND MASLOW'S HIERARCHY

The term was later used by Abraham Maslow in his article, A Theory of Human Motivation. Maslow explicitly defines self-actualization to be "the desire for self-fulfillment, namely the tendency for him [the individual] to become actualized in what he is potentially. This tendency might be phrased as the desire to become more and more what one is, to become everything that one is capable of becoming."[2] Maslow used the term self-actualization to describe a desire, not a driving force that could lead to realizing one's capabilities. Maslow did not feel that self-actualization determined one's life; rather, he felt that it gave the individual a desire, or motivation to achieve budding ambitions.[3] Maslow's usage of the term is now popular in modern psychology when discussing personality from the humanistic approach.

A basic definition from a typical college text book defines self-actualization according to Maslow simply as "the full realization of one's potential" without any mention of Goldstein.[3]

A more explicit definition of self-actualization according to Maslow is "intrinsic growth of what is already in the organism, or more accurately of what is the organism itself...self-actualization is growth-motivated rather than deficiency-motivated."[4] This explanation emphasizes the fact that self-actualization cannot normally be reached until other lower order necessities of Maslow's hierarchy of needs are satisfied. While Goldstein defined self-actualization as a driving force, Maslow uses the term to describe personal growth that takes place once lower order needs have been met.

Self-Actualized person according to Maslow "He possesses an unusual ability to detect the spurious, the fake, and the dishonest in personality and in general to judge the people correctly and efficiently"

Common traits amongst people who have reached self-actualization are: [5]

They embrace reality and facts rather than denying truth.

They are spontaneous.

They are interested in solving problems.

They are accepting of themselves and others and lack prejudice.

For Goldstein, it was a motive and, for Maslow, a level of development; for both, however, roughly the same kinds of qualities were expressed: independence, autonomy, a tendency to form few but deep friendships, a "philosophical" sense of humor, a tendency to resist outside pressures and a general transcendence of the environment rather than "coping" with it.[6]

Self-actualization resides at the top of Maslow's hierarchy of needs and is considered a part of the humanistic approach to personality. The humanistic approach is one of several methods used in psychology for studying, understanding, and evaluating personality. The humanistic approach was developed because other approaches, such as the psychodynamic approach made famous by Sigmund Freud, focused on unhealthy individuals that exhibited disturbed behavior.[3]

The humanistic approach focuses on healthy, motivated people and tries to determine how they define the self while maximizing their potential.[3]

Stemming from this branch of psychology is Maslow's hierarchy of needs. According to Maslow, people have lower order needs that in general must be fulfilled before high order needs can be satisfied. As a person moves up Maslow's hierarchy of needs, eventually they will reach the summit—self-actualization.[3] Maslow's hierarchy of needs begins with the most basic necessities deemed "the physiological needs" in which the individual will seek out items like food and water, and must be able to perform basic functions such as breathing and sleeping.[7] Once these needs have been met, a person can move on to fulfilling the "the safety needs", where they will attempt to obtain a sense of security, physical comforts and shelter, employment, and property.[7]

The next level is "the belongingness and love needs", where people will strive for social acceptance, affiliations, a sense of belongingness and being welcome, sexual intimacy, and perhaps a family.[7] Next are "the esteem needs", where the individual will desire a sense of competence, recognition of achievement by peers, and respect from others.[7] Some argue that once these needs are met, an individual is primed for self-actualization. Others argue that there are two more phases an individual must progress through before self-actualization can take place. These include "the cognitive needs", where a person will desire knowledge and an understanding of the world around them, and "the aesthetic needs" which include a need for "symmetry, order, and beauty".[3] Once all these needs have been satisfied, the final stage of Maslow's hierarchy—self-actualization—can take place.

[7] Classical Adlerian psychotherapy promotes this level of psychological development, utilizing the foundation of a 12-stage therapeutic model to realistically satisfy the basic needs, leading to an advanced stage of "meta-therapy," creative living, and self/other/task-actualization. Maslow's writings are used as inspirational resources. The key to Maslow's writings is understanding that there are no keys. Self-Actualization is predicated on the individual having their lower deficiency needs met. Once a person has moved through feeling and believing that they are deficient

APPENDIX III

Guide to Technical Report Writing

Contraire to popular belief, there is no ideal format, style or template for writing technical reports. This is so simply because there is no single list or requirement that is dictated by the need or purpose for writing all types of reports.

Some time ago I designed what I consider a good guide that provokes thought and at its best, serves as a grid for a sequence in writing reports. Over the years it has served me well as a guide for writing reports, and letters as well as other types of communications

THE INTRODUCTION

Establish the purpose for the writing. Tell what was done and how it was done. Give the salient results. Focus on the concept of what was done rather than expanded procedural details. For Example "This report documents work done to establish a method for... "We examined four factors believed to affect the..."

THE DISCUSSION

Explain the meaning of the results. Interpret the data and give the implications of your findings. Include tables and graphs. Do not hesitate to exercise your poetic license in this section. Explain your feelings about your findings. For example "Table I show…"

CONCLUSIONS

Give the results of the work in definite terms. Tie your conclusions to the introduction. Echo the strong points made in your discussion that deserve emphasis. Summarize unexpected results and explain variances.

APPENDIX IV

Public High School Graduation Rates—2006

ANNEX 9

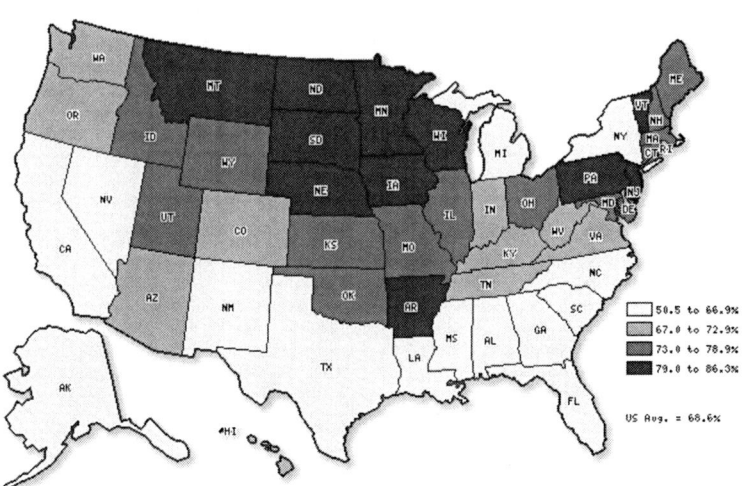

```
50.5 to 66.9%
67.0 to 72.9%
73.0 to 78.9%
79.0 to 86.3%

US Avg. = 68.6%
```

Source: Tom Mortenson, Postsecondary Opportunity

2008 GRADUATION RATES FOR RHODE ISLAND HIGH SCHOOLS

School ▾	Municipality	Type	Pct Graduated in 4 yrs	Pct Dropped Out by end of 4th year	Pct Completed GED within 4 yrs.	Pct Still in School after 4 yrs.	Pct Graduated in 4 yrs. (2007)	Pct Graduated in 5 yrs. (2008)	5-year graduation rate
Academy of Service	Providence	Urban	0.0%	78.6%	14.3%	7.1%	10.0%	20.0%	30.0%
Alvarez HS (Adelaide)	Providence	Urban	0.0%	62.1%	0.0%	37.9%	NA	NA	NA
BEACON Charter School	Charter	Other	60.0%	32.0%	6.0%	2.0%	57.7%	0.0%	57.7%
Barrington High School	Barrington	Suburban	95.7%	2.1%	1.7%	0.4%	95.2%	0.3%	95.5%
Blackstone Academy	Charter	Other	67.9%	7.1%	3.6%	21.4%	48.7%	11.5%	60.3%
Block Island School	New Shoreham	Suburban	100.0%	0.0%	0.0%	0.0%	*	*	*
Burrillville High School	Burrillville	Suburban	76.4%	12.4%	4.0%	7.1%	71.3%	2.2%	73.5%
Central Falls Senior HS	Central Falls	Urban	52.2%	30.0%	2.4%	15.5%	50.9%	4.2%	55.1%
Central High School	Providence	Urban	62.9%	29.4%	1.4%	6.4%	60.2%	2.8%	63.1%
Chariho Regional High School	Chariho	Suburban	86.0%	9.4%	0.7%	4.0%	80.9%	0.8%	81.7%
Classical High School	Providence	Urban	93.8%	4.0%	1.1%	1.1%	95.6%	1.1%	96.7%
Cooley/Health & Sci Tech	Providence	Urban	69.9%	24.4%	0.0%	5.8%	70.2%	6.0%	76.2%
Coventry High School	Coventry	Suburban	82.8%	11.4%	2.2%	3.7%	80.6%	0.0%	80.6%
Cranston High School East	Cranston	Urban Ring	83.4%	5.1%	8.3%	3.1%	76.4%	1.7%	78.1%
Cranston High School West	Cranston	Urban Ring	88.9%	7.3%	0.7%	3.2%	88.9%	0.8%	89.7%
Cumberland	Cumberland	Suburban	81.6%	9.3%	1.6%	7.5%	81.1%	0.0%	81.1%

School ▾	Municipality	Type	Pct Graduated in 4 yrs	Pct Dropped Out by end of 4th year	Pct Completed GED within 4 yrs.	Pct Still in School after 4 yrs.	Pct Graduated in 4 yrs. (2007)	Pct Graduated in 5 yrs. (2008)	5-year graduation rate
High School									
DCYF Alternative Ed	State-Operated	Other	3.8%	56.6%	24.7%	14.8%	13.0%	3.0%	16.0%
Davies Career-Tech	State-Operated	Other	67.6%	14.6%	3.2%	14.6%	72.4%	4.5%	76.9%
E-Cubed Academy	Providence	Urban	60.0%	29.5%	2.9%	7.6%	57.3%	7.8%	65.0%
E. Greenwich High School	E. Greenwich	Suburban	94.4%	1.5%	1.5%	2.6%	94.5%	0.0%	94.5%
E. Providence High School	E. Providence	Urban Ring	76.8%	17.5%	1.1%	4.5%	69.0%	3.7%	72.7%
Exeter-W. Greenwich HS	Ex-W. Greenwich	Suburban	87.6%	5.2%	2.6%	4.7%	87.1%	0.5%	87.6%
Feinstein High School	Providence	Urban	56.2%	26.7%	3.8%	13.3%	56.6%	13.2%	69.8%
Hope Arts School	Providence	Urban	50.8%	38.1%	4.0%	7.1%	55.6%	6.0%	61.7%
Hope Info Tech School	Providence	Urban	48.6%	39.2%	2.7%	9.5%	54.2%	2.1%	56.3%
Hope Leadership School	Providence	Urban	53.4%	32.3%	2.3%	12.0%	54.5%	3.8%	58.3%
Johnston Senior High School	Johnston	Urban Ring	78.6%	6.3%	8.7%	6.3%	61.8%	2.9%	64.6%
Lincoln Senior High School	Lincoln	Suburban	83.7%	12.1%	2.3%	2.0%	86.1%	1.4%	87.5%
Middletown High School	Middletown	Suburban	84.2%	5.9%	3.9%	5.9%	81.3%	1.5%	82.8%
Mount Pleasant High School	Providence	Urban	65.0%	22.6%	1.7%	10.8%	56.7%	3.8%	60.5%
Mt. Hope	Bristol	Suburban	80.5%	10.4%	2.0%	7.2%	74.8%	4.2%	79.0%

149

School	Municipality	Type	Pct Graduated in 4 yrs	Pct Dropped Out by end of 4th year	Pct Completed GED within 4 yrs.	Pct Still in School after 4 yrs.	Pct Graduated in 4 yrs. (2007)	Pct Graduated in 5 yrs. (2008)	5-year graduation rate
High School	Warren								
N. Kingstown Senior HS	N. Kingstown	Suburban	89.3%	5.9%	2.1%	2.7%	91.4%	0.0%	91.4%
N. Providence HS	N. Providence	Urban Ring	88.8%	4.6%	1.1%	5.6%	87.6%	1.2%	88.8%
N. Smithfield High School	N. Smithfield	Suburban	89.5%	1.6%	6.5%	2.4%	87.2%	2.3%	89.5%
NE Laborers' Career Academy	Cranston	Urban Ring	56.3%	19.4%	5.8%	18.4%	77.4%	3.2%	80.6%
Narragansett High School	Narragansett	Suburban	95.6%	2.7%	0.9%	0.9%	88.7%	1.4%	90.1%
Pilgrim High School	Warwick	Urban Ring	71.3%	13.6%	4.4%	10.7%	64.5%	1.9%	66.4%
Ponaganset High School	Foster-Glocester	Suburban	87.0%	7.7%	2.7%	2.7%	93.8%	1.4%	95.2%
Portsmouth High School	Portsmouth	Suburban	86.6%	4.6%	6.0%	2.8%	87.9%	1.4%	89.3%
Prov Acad of Int'l Studies	Providence	Urban	72.7%	21.7%	2.8%	2.8%	67.4%	1.6%	69.0%
R.I. School for the Deaf	State-Operated	Other	*	*	*	*	*	*	*
R.Y.S.E.	Chariho	Suburban	36.4%	36.4%	18.2%	9.1%	47.1%	11.8%	58.8%
Rogers High School	Newport	Urban Ring	66.7%	21.5%	3.2%	8.6%	62.1%	3.1%	65.2%
S. Kingstown High School	S. Kingstown	Suburban	87.7%	7.3%	2.0%	3.0%	85.2%	1.9%	87.0%
Scituate High School	Scituate	Suburban	84.1%	8.5%	3.7%	3.7%	85.1%	2.0%	87.2%
Shea Senior High School	Pawtucket	Urban	57.0%	26.6%	1.9%	14.6%	50.4%	3.6%	54.0%
Smithfield Senior High School	Smithfield	Suburban	88.7%	5.6%	1.4%	4.2%	85.9%	0.0%	85.9%
Textron	Providence	Urban	100.0%	0.0%	0.0%	0.0%	93.3%	0.0%	93.3%
The Met	State-	Other	74.1%	12.7%	2.0%	11.2%	82.1%	8.5%	90.5%

150

School ▾	Municipality	Type	Pct Graduated in 4 yrs	Pct Dropped Out by end of 4th year	Pct Completed GED within 4 yrs.	Pct Still in School after 4 yrs.	Pct Graduated in 4 yrs. (2007)	Pct Graduated in 5 yrs. (2008)	5-year graduation rate
	Operated								
Times2 Academy	Providence	Urban	100.0%	0.0%	0.0%	0.0%	100.0%	0.0%	100.0%
Tiverton High School	Tiverton	Suburban	82.8%	9.1%	5.1%	3.0%	80.4%	1.5%	81.9%
Toll Gate High School	Warwick	Urban Ring	77.2%	12.9%	3.0%	6.9%	68.8%	0.9%	69.7%
Tolman Senior High School	Pawtucket	Urban	58.2%	24.3%	9.0%	8.5%	46.2%	2.1%	48.3%
W. Warwick Senior HS	W. Warwick	Urban Ring	68.4%	19.0%	3.7%	8.8%	66.6%	3.6%	70.1%
Warwick Veterans Memorial HS	Warwick	Urban Ring	70.4%	12.3%	4.9%	12.3%	66.7%	2.6%	69.3%
Westerly High School	Westerly	Suburban	89.2%	5.2%	1.7%	3.8%	90.5%	2.9%	93.4%
Woonsocket High School	Woonsocket	Urban	60.2%	27.6%	3.3%	8.9%	54.1%	2.5%	56.6%

Note: NA: Not computed; school did not exist. * - Too few students to report rates

Source: Information Works! School Year 2007-08

projo.com / Timothy C. Barmann

EXAMPLES OF DISCIPLINE REFERRALS

Student X

On Tuesday, the class was taking their final semester assessment exam. Student X, a 10th grader was consistently disturbing the class. He was told to report to the principle and immediately left the class but returned about 15 minutes later. He immediately left the class a second time. Shortly thereafter I noticed a stack of exam papers had been removed from my desk. One of my students informed me that student X had taken the papers.

I informed a hall monitors that my test papers were missing and student X was suspect. He was asked to search for him.

After a few minutes, the monitor returned with Student X"s book bag. He informed me that they had found Student X with test papers but he would not surrender them. He asked that I keep the book bag because he felt he would return for it. I notice the partially opened book bag contained a microscope of the type used in biology classes.

Shortly, Student X appeared at the classroom door, aggressively shelved me out of his path, grabbed the book bag and ran rapidly down the back stairs. I called for him to stop, but he continued to run. My 6-6 chemistry class witnesses the episode with the book bag.

A few minutes the hall monitor returned the test papers to me and I informed him that Student X had grabbed his book bag containing a microscope and ran down the back stairs. He was also informed that a telephone hand set was also missing from my classroom. The telephone hand set was later found in the principal's office and a microscope was found in the trash dumpster.

DISCIPLINE REFERRAL   *Student Y*

Student Y was noted standing in the hall well pass the start of class time .He had been advised several times to report to class and remove his head gear. The principal passed and also advised the student to remove his head gear and report to class. Eventually, student Y reported to class but did not remove his head gear. After considerable debate and class disruptions he removed his head gear.

Student Y and several other boys were sent out of class to get their text book. Student Y returned about 15 minutes after the other boys, again wearing his head gear. Student Y continued to disrupt the class and was asked to leave and report to the principal. He refused to leave the class and continued to disrupt the class. He called me stupid and several other disrespectful names.

At this point student y was about 15 additional minutes into serious class disruptions. The principal was summoned and asked to remove him from the class.

On past occasions student y has been disruptive in class. His actions on this occasion appeared erratic and somewhat hostile.

Prior to this incidence, his Father was contacted and advised of his conduct in class. His Father told me that prior to this year Student Y was a model student and was never before in trouble. But this year was different. He advised me that he would speak to him.

EXAMPLE OF STUDENT REFERRAL *Student Z*

DISCIPLINE REFERRAL

December 2,
To: Principle
From: John V. Patrick
In preparation for taking a quiz, Student Z had moved his seat from its normal position to a more crowded table, even though the class was advised to spread out. Steven refused to move his seat and began to use foul language, specifically directed at me.

Steven was asked to leave the class and refused. His foul language intensified. The principle was summoned to the class and witnessed additional foul language directed at me. On his way out of the class with the principle, he made a threatening gesture at me while continuing the foul language.

APPENDIX V

Following is a revised model for writing your final report on the water-drop penny project.

INTRODUCTION

The object of this project was to identity variables for placing the maximum number of water drop. Table 1 attached shows the variables studied in a two level-four factor factorial experiment. The results showed————. Explain your salient results.

DISCUSSION

Table II, attached, shows the experimental outline and the results. The data was analyzed by——————————.*Explain what you did, how you analyzed the data and the meaning of the results of your analysis. Explain any inconsistencies. Give your opinion of the data in technical terms. Include statistical averages in your analysis of each variable. Use tables to show the explanation of your analysis. Consult with your math and or physic teacher, if necessary, or perhaps consult the internet (key word factorial experiments) or your English teacher, to help interpret the data. Discuss the mean, mode and averages involved with each variable. Remember you tested each variable eight times. And, do not forget to use your poetic license. You did the work. Be proud of it. Use your guide for technical report writing.*

CONCLUSIONS

Keep it simple but accurate and direct. You might consider using bullets to give your conclusions.

Your science rubric, attached, applies to this project and it is a portfolio project.

APPENDIX VI

Directions to a Deficient Student Wanting to Graduate

June 16,
To: Student Wanting to Graduate
Subject: Special Project, Chemistry A
You have indicated that you are considering a career in hair science. You have also expressed a desire to improve your chemistry grade. The following is criteria by which you may do so. Your rubric for "Structured Inquiry" applies to this assignment.

Write a ten-page report on hair chemistry. The report must include the following related sub-tropics.
General hair chemistry—analytical, physical and structural aspects of hair.
Hair color and coloring.
Hair growth and the factors that may affect hair growth.
The chemistry of hair care products including shampoos and conditioners.
Artificial hair and hair implants.
Diseases of the scalp

I have attaches a copy of a Google web index on hair chemistry. It may help you with your efforts. This report is due no later than 24 hours before graduation but may be submitted before then.

Good luck,

About the Author

John V. Patrick was born in GalvestonTexas, the fifth of six children born to Ollie and Virginia Patrick. He attended a segregated high school and college, receiving a BS degree in chemistry, minor in mathematics and a commission in the US Army from PrairieViewA&MUniversity. His interest in teaching children begin while serving in the army where he gained special recognition for his contribution in producing the company with the highest proficiency score ever for an advanced infantry basic training company.

After the army, he taught mathematics and science at a regional New JerseyJr/ Sr high School. After a short stint, the lure of money led him to an extensive career as a research chemist in industry where he rose thru senior chemist, technical director, and manager of manufacturing. While working in industry, he developed his skills from graduate courses in management, finance, psychology, experimental design and analysis of variance.

He later became a Rhode Island certified teacher of chemistry where he practiced for 12 years before retiring.

His interest in education was jolted when he returned to teaching from industry after a 35 year hiatus and noticed the quality of education had changed and was being hampered by an agglomeration of issues. Using his background in research and development coupled with his background with

159

young people in the military, in the classroom 35 years ago in manufacturing and more recently and again in the classroom, he rapidly developed theories and more importantly new rationale about the big dilemma of failing schools—their causes and solutions.

Would you like to see your manuscript become a book?

If you are interested in becoming a PublishAmerica author, please submit your manuscript for possible publication to us at:

acquisitions@publishamerica.com

You may also mail in your manuscript to:

**PublishAmerica
PO Box 151
Frederick, MD 21705**

www.publishamerica.com

Breinigsville, PA USA
08 April 2011
259491BV00001B/8/P